Oliver's Crossing

A NOVEL OF CADES COVE

Catherine Astl

BRIGHTON PUBLISHING LLC
435 N. HARRIS DRIVE
MESA, AZ 85203

Oliver's Crossing
A Novel of Cades Cove

Catherine Astl

Brighton Publishing LLC
435 N. Harris Drive
Mesa, AZ 85203

www.BrightonPublishing.com

Copyright © 2020

ISBN: 978-1-62183-578-3

Printed in the United States of America

First Edition

Cover Design: Tom Rodriguez

Also by Catherine Astl

NON-FICTION:

Behind the Bar—Inside the Paralegal Profession

Behind the Bar—From Intake to Trial

FICTION:

Three Gates

The Colonists

Dedication

TO THE PEOPLE OF CADES COVE.

ᑕ᠊ᔆᐤAcknowledgments᠊ᕽᐤ

No author of historical fiction can do it alone. I owe a world of appreciation to the authors of the materials and sources I have used in this work.

I wish to especially point out Durwood Dunn's wonderful book, *Cades Cove, The Life and Death of a Southern Appalachian Community*, and A. Randolph Shields' book, *A Cades Cove Story*. So much of these books are contained within, and these played a very large role in how I made the story come to life. John W. Oliver's memoir also played a huge role, as did Ferguson Realty's wonderfully detailed story, *Cades Cove*.

As is the case in historical fiction novels, there are no footnotes or citations for these direct quotes; however, I do wish to note that there are many places in this book where I have quoted directly from these sources. Those places are designated in quotation marks or italics.

Additionally, though there are numerous photographs of Cades Cove's history in archives, I chose to include photographs from the modern day Cove. This choice was so readers could connect the story with what they can actually see today. I feel this choice brings together the best of both worlds–of the story and of the national park.

I wish to thank my parents, Nick and Cathryn Abernathy, for loving me unconditionally, supporting me always, and instilling a work ethic like no other. My mother, whose personal library houses 1,500 books and then some, planted in me the love of reading and writing from a very early age. I also wish to thank my sister and nephews, Caroline Fielding and Bryan and Steven Fielding, who listened to the progress of this book and supported me throughout. I thank Scott Stevison who helped me with rifle research and helped me dig deeper into the naming of rifles, but who also patiently listened to portions of this book many a night. Finally, I thank my dearest son, Dean Alexander Astl, who captured the cove so beautifully in his pictures (and, he's only 13!) and for supporting me throughout this entire process. I love you, my dear son ...to the moon and back a million times.

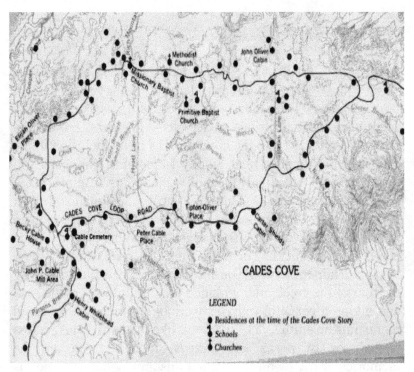

(SOURCE: THE NATIONAL PARK SERVICE, CULTURAL LANDSCAPES INVENTORY)

Preface and Author's Note

Cades Cove is a place where the soul knows it is home. An ancient valley in Eastern Tennessee, its mountain peaks saw a successful and industrious society for 119 years. From John Oliver's first steps into the cove in 1818 to its inclusion in the 1937 opening of the Great Smoky Mountains National Park, this quiet and stunningly beautiful place has inspired many who have vacationed in America's most visited national park. Perhaps you've driven the loop motor trail, and have walked into the preserved cabins alongside. Maybe you've been involved in a "ruckus" or traffic jam if a bear was anywhere nearby. I hope many of you have experienced picnicking by the roar of the creek after a night's rain, or pulling off the road and hiking a peaceful trail, or overlooking the most beautiful mountains on earth—ones that look like the earth is an endless jagged sea of peaks and valleys. Indeed, these are the memories of my own life, visiting this area countless times as a little girl, and later, as a mother, bringing my own son to cherish the scenery and history.

But even as a young girl, I could feel the magic in the mountains and especially in Cades Cove. I learned a bit about it. I knew people had actually lived here. We were asked by rangers and brochures alike to imagine the area loaded with farms and homesteads. Blurbs of the stories were told in guidebooks, in memoirs, on plaques outside historic structures, and in many great histories of the area. Yet, I always wanted to know more. I wanted to discover and bring to life their way of life. What made the people of Cades Cove so special? What makes their history so magical and inspiring?

Through exhaustive research, I present to you this book, which I believe, answers those questions and then some. This is a work of fiction, but the people described are real, as are all of the major events. Within these pages are historical facts and exact quotes taken from some of the best sources, some from the very memoirs of the people themselves.

This is my third novel and fifth book; it was wonderful to research and write, me being a huge history buff and feeling such a personal connection to the cove. I've written my entire life, but this project was different; a place I knew so well felt, at different times, like a stranger, a best friend, a short-term visitor, and something I could never live without. There were some days that the words were simply dictated to me by the mountains themselves, none of my own thoughts interfering.

But my own thoughts did interfere, of course. Every writer has that inner voice that's just their own, and can never be shut off. And so, I acknowledge that while I took meticulous pride in conducting research for this book, all errors and omissions and mistakes and liberties are my own. I own those faults in full.

My hope is that this book honors the memories of the people of Cades Cove and their unique and special way of life, and inspires you to visit or return to the most ideal and perfect place on earth.

Chapter One

1818—JOHN AND LUCRETIA OLIVER

The eagle flew all day. When he finally perched on his favorite branch, high up in the tree, he fluffed his wings and settled to watch the horse pulling an old wooden wagon. It was rickety and he watched as the people bounced to and fro, as if waltzing with the wind. The large tan-colored animal was excited; the eagle picking up on the four-legged horse's emotions. Perhaps there was some anxiety too, for its tail flicked violently. The keen avian eyes zeroed in on the woman with the egg on her belly. He wondered why they didn't just lay eggs like he and his mate. Sit on them, keep them warm. Why was there an egg in the middle of her body? Wondering about the ways of humans, he turned his attention to the man. Not too tall, brown hair and thin, but sturdy, the man yelled, "Whoa!" pulling back on two thick leather strips that seemed to stop both horse and wagon. Stepping down, the man placed his fists into his back, trying to stretch the journey out of his muscles, and looked up. What was it he saw? The man had stood stock still, staring. One of nature's sharpest eyes caught the gleam in the man's soul; seared right through the feathery creature's breast.

That man has just come home.

It was late in the fall of 1818 and John Oliver couldn't believe his eyes. Scalloped peaks merged with the endless sky, their pensive caps of snow on constant watch. Treed slopes slid into the untouched basin from all sides. He looked out at the vast valley in amazement, the valley that was in the middle of it all. Then, his gaze swiveled westward to a stand of trees. He blinked, taking a few steps for a better view. *Yes, there it is.* He knew it instinctually—the very tree he would be laid to rest under—the largest and broadest of chestnuts, its leafy shadows providing permanent lacy layers below. *This is the place I will die.* He joyfully swept his gaze over his entire final resting place, a coffin of satiny breezes and fertile air, trying to take it all in. It was five miles long and two miles wide. But it was too much to map in the mind's eye in just a few minutes' time. He would need a lifetime, starting now. Home—he'd never really had one. Not one of his own anyway.

"Quite the burial place," his wife observed, reading his thoughts—an easy feat, for he made no secret of what he was seeking as they embarked on their journey. She too was working out the journey's kinks in her back and neck, placing one hand to her neck; both hands to the sky. *It feels so good to stretch!* Weary, she stood with John, trying to take it all in.

John's eyes crinkled with a laugh. *Quite perfect*, he thought happily, as he continued to look out at the forested fields. "My God, look at this ...."

Untamed land tucked neatly into a valley—an elliptical cove teaming with creeks, game, rich soil, and ghosts of the past. John, a history buff, already knew that the curious Spaniard Hernando De Soto saw this land way back in 1540, and he had even met the native Cherokees who called the cove, "Tsiyahi, or 'place of the river otter." From what he'd heard of the legends, these feather-and-leather laden Indians hunted here in the summer, but never actually lived in the cove. John had certainly done his research on what would be his new home and knew that De Soto had marveled at this isolated sloping gorge protected on all sides by mountains worn down over millennia. *That imagery alone could tug at a man's ambition*, John had thought.

When the exploring Spaniards came across this area, De Soto had carefully entered detailed accounts of this land, surveying and documenting its vegetation, climate and such for future botanists, and for the scattering of temporary settlements that arose here, centuries before today, the day that John Oliver arrived.

As he sunk his worn boots into the plush dirt and pine needles of this particular sheltered mouth of the mountains, his young face, lightly lined from the sun, saw where his bright future finally greeted his dreams. Yet John knew all too well that bright beacons shine only for the tough and hearty, only for those who could see through the thick brush, the beauty and potential of this place, this vast basin surrounded by peaks that began 400-plus million years ago. He was always fascinated with facts, geology and history. Not that he read books ...he couldn't read or write very well, but he'd heard it all by talking to the right people. By living through others' experiences and asking questions about the things, events, people, life these mountains have seen, all through keen eyes that sparkle or weep, depending on the era.

The mountains are alive, and had thoughts of their own that day ...*water shaped us, freezing and freezing again, thawing, running water carving out our features, the elements hacking us to pieces, until, one day, here in 1818, we are left with gentle slopes on our tops, feeling the wind down our backbones. We are not finished and have yet many lives to live. Still, we evolve, and now, this newest appearance of humans—the smallest group yet—is here to move amongst our spines, our bones, our hearts. And, we will do what we always do: sit here, majestically, and watch it all play out.*

Carved and flattened by wind and water over millions of years, a lush, fertile valley had formed; perfect conditions for any human that happened upon the place. There hadn't been many thus far, as the mountains knew, but John already sensed that his own future burial place would also house some of the luckiest, perhaps the most ill-fated, people to ever live. They would remain here, forever, right here, even right this very moment; teaching the lessons of hardships, experiences, celebrations, deaths, lives. He knew he would not be alone for he saw it all before him, immediately and perfectly in his mind's eye. The future inhabitants who would live here, tucked away from progress, would find homes in the one place where their souls wouldn't be recognized as separate from the land. Meadows and mountains would draw them in, and no matter if they stayed forever, or made an eventual life somewhere else, the story of one mountain pioneer reaching a crucial crossing in life, in a place known as Cades Cove, would bring forth a way of life that would leave an entire world inspired. And, as John Oliver crossed the mountains and arrived in the breezes of the cove, crossed from his old life into the new, crossed his fear with freedom, and crossed every limb of his strong body for luck, the story began.

Joshua Jobe had persuaded John and Lucretia Oliver to move from Carter County to the cove. Jobe, their friend and neighbor when they all lived in the northeast corner of Tennessee, knew John well; John rarely, but poignantly lamenting, "I grew up so poor, I want -*need*- more. Something to call my own." Jobe knew his friend would jump at the chance to own his own land, build his own house, and raise a family in a truly new place. Something that may be too hard to do in his current situation.

"This new place don't really yet have any formal name; the Cherokees call it something for one of the wives of a Chief ...I forget just what ...we won't worry about that right now. I don't even know 'bout the relinquishing their claim to these lands—they have no claims 'far as I know, but I have visited the cove myself, seen it with my own eyes, and I declare, it's the opportunity of a lifetime." Jobe was very convincing, even passionate about this rare and new opportunity.

Tennessee had just become a state in 1796—a mere twenty-two years before Jobe told John all about the little valley tucked under its right flank, a little south of where they all lived. Land rights didn't matter? He could take what he saw as the best land? Have his own farm?

It did not take much convincing.

"I mean it, John. I'm moving my own family there, soon as I can get things squared away."

"There's truly land for the taking?"

"Yes. I've not seen no Cherokees, and even so, they ain't gonna mess with you. They don't live there. Maybe they'll go in to hunt once in a while. May scatter some crops 'round the area. But nothing permanent. No claims. They pass through. But I ain't ever seen one stick around. Never."

"And, there's more of us coming?"

"Oh yessir, John. I already told you ...I'm bringing my own family. Better cherish it while you can ...we'll all be moving in on y'all very soon!" He chuckled. "Neighbors, we'll be ...friendly ones. We're gonna make our own community where we'll all grow healthy and be happy. Have our own land. Youngins can marry each other and we can all help each other grow old." He chuckled. "Ain't that what our Constitution says we should do? Life ...pursuit of happiness? Liberty?"

And so, the small clan of Olivers packed up their belongings, took the only route going down Tennessee's southeast boundary, and showed up in one of its most beautiful, treacherous, isolated, and soul-lifting mountain valleys that had ever embraced human life.

"The East end here seems best. It's higher and drier than the lower end." John was saying to his wife, after arriving with their horse and wagon, seeing his own burial place, and returning from a quick reconnaissance of their choice of stopping place. He wished he could take it all in for more than a moment, but he couldn't stand in awe forever at the beauty before him. He had to get moving. Though it was still early, days wait for no one; the sun dips behind mountains with astonishing speed, covering themselves in the darkest of cloaks.

Boots muddy, and faces sweaty, the husband and wife had arrived and were eager to get settled in the cove, well away from the swampy areas. John knew the first few days would have him cutting trees and building a house. Priorities here were simple and clear.

"The garden needs to be planted, but it's so late in the season..." Luraney trailed thinking and looking around at her new homeland. They had certainly thought about the time of year they chose to travel here—late, late fall. Not ideal for sure, but they knew they'd have help shortly. Jobe was coming back and with plenty of new settlers.

"I saw from the wagon, there's some blackberries and blueberries in them fields over there, and I am sure there's some chestnuts up that hill." John pointed to the hilly area to his right. He had glimpsed some game on their ride into the valley—a rabbit, a deer—and he was feeling confident about their chances. Lucretia, also known as Lurena, or Luraney, as he called her, wasn't feeling quite so hopeful. She knew the garden was the most important thing to start, but it was way too late in the season to plant anything, much less the big crops of wheat and corn. For now, they'd have to make do with hunting and gathering, and the meager food they had brought with them. Besides, Jobe will be back. He promised to bring food and provisions.

She roamed around, boots crunching fallen dead leaves, lost in her thoughts. She was a pretty young woman, some might call a bit plain, but her eyes sparkled with intelligence and that nice mixture of grit and softness. Those eyes looked hard at this new reality, but then brightened when she saw apples hanging down trees. *I thought Jobe told us there was no fruit trees here ...but here are some. Just a few, true, but they're surely apples. I wonder how they got here.*

She immediately ran back to the wagon to grab her large basket. Ran may be a strong word—she waddled, for Luraney was pregnant with their second baby. Their first child, a daughter they'd named Mary Oliver, was born last year, on July 18, 1817. What a day that was! Luraney reminisced for a moment, remembering the squirmy little human emerging into the world, and she smiled in the middle of a refreshing breeze coming through the trees, the apples waving to her. She loved being a mother. Mary, who they nicknamed Polly, was now slung low on her hip, in a homemade quilted sling, sleeping away her parents' new adventures.

While Luraney walked with her child, who remained lulled into a light sleep, her reflections moved from her daughter to their trip and, then, to herself. Ten days along the

Indian Warpath, a well-traveled trail. *Not even a road,* she thought. *A long way from where I thought I'd be.* She sighed, shifting Polly to her other side, all the better to reach up for the ripest fruits.

Luraney was a "bound girl" when she met John, her parents having died with no one else to take care of her. *Well, died may not exactly be true,* she huffed to herself, wondering what her real story was. Someone had once told her that her father, John Frazier, had placed at least two of his offspring—one of them herself—on public suffrage, which was the welfare system of the day, and there was no reason to believe he wasn't still alive. As for her mother ...she simply had no idea.

Volunteer families, bound by court order, took care of children on public suffrage and many likened the living conditions to being an indentured servant, until into young adulthood. The "someone" who told Luraney all about her background wasn't intending to be cruel to her. Family ties were crucial in society, and the "someone" felt it important for Luraney to know. And it *was* important to know that her options were limited; it was the only way for Luraney to understand, with crystal clarity, that the only way out of her situation was to marry. Marry as best she can. Wasn't that the chief occupation for women in this time period, and throughout history?

"He's very nice. Has a pleasant face and character. Dirt poor—ain't we all. But he's a very hard worker." Luraney said to one of her few friends. "And he's willing to marry me. I'm bound you know." She almost whispered it, ashamed.

Then she sighed deeply. "Our courting will be cut short. He's going to the War."

"Well, is he worth waiting for? All the Tennessee men are going to war. Who will come back? That's who you'll marry." Luraney's friend was practical and realistic, looking for a man to marry for herself. Women needed to marry. There were very few other choices. Besides, without a husband and children, what in the world would they do with their lives?

And so, the women passed the time, doing what women did throughout history: waited for men to stop fighting. Sewing, cooking, gossiping, weeding the gardens, piano playing, reading, raising children if there were any yet. If not, they'd help with aunts', sisters' and friends' children. Tending whatever chores were necessary, wondering what would become of them, and asking the perpetual question: why couldn't men talk it out like most women did? Different ways of resolving conflict have always been one of the biggest differences between the sexes.

"I think they need it—war, that is. Otherwise, everythin' would stay the same."

Luraney nodded her head in agreement.

"There would be no need for advancement or progress. Nothin' new would happen ...war forces us to be enterprisin'. Not nearly enough jobs if not for war. And ...men—they need to prove themselves. Hard to do without a gun."

"Or a sword or knife." Luraney mused to her friend while endlessly talking about waiting and waiting for men to cease fighting long enough to enjoy all other aspects of life.

But Luraney was especially good at waiting and, with a stockpile of quilts, an arsenal of very practical skills, and a good head on her shoulders, she did marry John after he marched a long way, from East Tennessee and over and down to Alabama—"the Horseshoe Bend area" - as he told her. "I even fought with guys under General Jackson," he proudly boasted.

"Andrew Jackson?"

"Yes ma'am." Smiling at Luraney as he simply showed up one evening, back from war, talkative and excited, and not in the mood to waste any more time. They had exchanged very few letters during his time at war, very little communication had occurred, but now he was here and anxious to get on with his life.

"I'm back. And I want to marry you."

It was as simple as that. No reigniting of the courtship, no more rare letters from the field, wasn't interested in chats by the fire, or even long walks to reacquaint themselves; it was now all business. After all, war has a way of taking the romance out of life. War is often written about, fantasized about, glorified ...but any man who actually goes to war soon realizes there is no majesty, no relishing or prideful boasting that one gains. Nothing but a respectful sorrow. No shame or regrets mind you, for John knew in his heart that the cause was just, but he was ready to put the fighting behind him, settle down, and raise a family. But where? He was so poor. And his work, as he explained it, was simple and would get him nowhere. "I am a collier, working with coal, cutting firewood and burnin' it to create coke to fuel iron smelters ...it's dirty. And it ain't paying." He looked right into his wife's eyes. "And it never will." He looked around their tiny room, elbows on his knees, hands to his mouth, itching like crazy inside, now that he may have found his way out.

"I have ambition. Lots of it. I just need the proper place for its outlay." John paused for a moment, readying his argument.

"And Jobe—he told me the proper place, so to speak. Listen to what he tells me...."

Luraney listened to her husband, though this wasn't the first time he'd mentioned it. But John was talking more seriously now, with more detail, like this whole plan was a given.

"He said, there's a place called Cades Cove, which is very fertile...."

"Wait, I thought it didn't have a name!" Already picking holes in the argument—didn't Jobe say he wasn't sure of the name? But right now, *she* wasn't so sure about moving. Parts of her bloomed with anticipation and opportunity; parts sunk with absolute fear. After having such an unstable childhood, she just wanted to stay in one place. *But where was that place? Was it here? Or somewhere else?*

"Well, it don't. Have a name, that is. Not formally anyways...so they say. They call it something for some Indian Chief's wife—Kate somethin' or other. But listen, Luraney, the name's not important."

And now she was actually here, standing in their new land of opportunity. Luraney stared at the apples, her little Polly in the sling, and remembered the rest of the conversations like it was yesterday—both John and Jobe so excited....

"We can plant crops—corn, wheat; grow just about anything, lots of game...I'm goin' there myself. Why not come with me?" Joshua Jobe tried hard to convince the young married couple, but he found it wasn't too difficult. He knew it wouldn't be, for John was seeking something new, something with enthusiasm and opportunity for him and Luraney. Jobe wasn't shocked at all when John immediately liked and agreed to the idea. *He'd barely even asked me what I thought,* she recalled.

11

Jobe didn't mention the Indian massacres during the moments of convincing the Olivers, nor the fact that he had seen Indian hostility firsthand and, of course, knew about the Kirk Family Massacre in 1788—one woman and ten children killed by Indians ...an unbelievable loss. *Because the Cherokee said we was on their land, illegally.* That reason was the official motive for the Indians' attack, and, though most of the white men felt the same way and many would've done the same thing if they found anyone on *their* land illegally, they still denigrated the savage, uncivilized red and brown men for their actions.

This event was years ago now, but fresh in many living memories. Jobe was pretty sure that Luraney knew about it; her face betrayed her trying to remember the vague memory of the story, but Jobe did not dare say anything. No, no need to mention that. That's old news already. Besides, she never mentioned or asked about the Indians. Not much anyway. *Those questions are best answered by John anyways, he knows her enough that he can say it in a way so she's not discouraged before she even gets here.* Jobe quickly moved on with the many attributes of the cove, seeing the Olivers' smiles and souls—especially John's—rise with hope and opportunity.

Poor. When that description comes to mind, what do you see? Feel? Have you ever been so poor that you starved? That you were in real danger of losing your life? The Olivers were very, very poor and were actually struggling to live. They knew they'd never make it if they just stood still; never enough to eat, never a good shelter to come home to. Cold. Not enough clothes. Never enough ...very, very cold all the time.

"So just 'bout anything will be better than this smoky, burning, backbreaking and sweaty work of a collier. Diggin' and dealin' with coal day in and day out. It's not me." John had whispered to his wife, trying to keep as warm as possible under threadbare quilts, their stomachs empty and crying out in pain. After conversing about the opportunity and move, briefly and with surprisingly little questioning of choices— because what were they losing really?—John and Luraney Oliver loaded up what little they had: *"the clothes on our backs, a rifle, a good axe, knives, a fork and spoon, a Dutch oven, a skillet, a few blankets, and fire-starting material. Maybe a little sack of flour and sugar. Salt. Just a bit. The lowest supply of coffee one can imagine.*

And so, the little family set out, filled with excitement and more than a little trepidation. Yet, this was their hope— perhaps only hope—of escaping the blackened life of a very poor collier.

Ten days later, the young Olivers, the first documented and permanent white settlers of the area entered the cove. The eagle watched as the wagon pulled by the sturdy young horse—the family's only other possession—lurched to a stop. After such a rutted and bumpy journey, they still felt like they were moving, and she remembered swaying a bit as she began to disembark. Felt a bit queasy actually. Dizzy for a few moments. Deep breaths were taken—in through the nose, out through the mouth—stomachs calmed, and the horse snorted the dust from its nose. The couple gripped each other's hands, looked around, listened, and heard ...nothing.

Luraney stepped down, stretched, putting her hands on her hips and gasped at a scene of the rarest beauty. She stared at a basin of fertile land that—she could just picture it—would be their home and where others would come and surround each other's lives. Encasing that dip of fertile land, that valley where they could grow their food and family, were the most stunning, softly peaked mountains she'd ever seen. The sight of such rare beauty immediately lifted her spirits, and a keen sense of adventure enveloped her for the first time. "Maybe this will be wonderful," she fervently hoped. She was both excited and anxious—more excited now that she was actually standing here—and for the first time perhaps, truly felt her husband's hopes and dreams. *They will come true. But some suffering will come no doubt.* Remaining pragmatic as was her nature, her thoughts interrupted her enthusiasm.

Joshua Jobe had escorted them as far as he could, as far as his time allowed—after all, it had been ten days. He had to get back to his own business. He left the Olivers less than a mile or so before they emerged through the mountain pass into their new home. "Go on ahead, it's dead straight ahead. The road goes right in." He waved them on, turned back and promised, *"I'll be back in the morning."* He wasn't going all the way home—that would take ten days there and ten days back. But he had other business in the nearby area, and he planned on coming back that very next day, to survey more thoroughly, before then settling his own family in the coming weeks. The Olivers' friend galloped away and left them for that first night in the beautiful, chilly, lonely cove.

Stepping down from the wagon, she covered her little Polly, who had endured the trip like a hardy pioneer. She rubbed her belly, hoping her next baby would be born with the same hardiness. Looking around, the trees waved their welcome, and songs of the birds danced through the wind. An eagle swooped down, a symbol of strength and hope. The majestic bird eyed the humans, and their paraphernalia bursting out of and hanging on a wooden wagon. His nest provided a great vantage point to watch. The egg on the woman's belly was so small ...yet he could see it with those keen eyes. Strange... The eagle turned his attention to the man, who seemed very, very busy in the mind. *He's found his home. Now, he has to figure out how to survive here.*

The air was cool, but not yet crisp. Leaves crunched underfoot, but there was a surprising amount of foliage still left on the trees. And it hadn't rained. Perfect. She sighed with relief with getting out of the wagon, and for finally seeing her new life. She saw in her husband's eyes that he had seen his home. *Am I home?* It was still a question, but one she felt would be answered in due time. "Yes, this could be home. It *is* home, for now. Maybe forever."

Holding back just then, she thought to herself, *but we will see.* She had gasped at the rare beauty of this place, yet still had lots and lots of reservations about this move. More so now that they'd arrived ...even with Jobe, they'd still be largely alone. For a while anyway. Until spring came perhaps. And it was cold; winter hadn't even arrived yet. The winds blew down the slopes, through the gorges, and into their lungs and bones. It was wild here. Nothing for miles. But Jobe *was* coming back ...wasn't he?

Surely he would. And, then, they would have help.

Suddenly, she lifted herself out of her thoughts. She had to get moving. For there was nothing *immediate* that had to be done—they had some food for themselves, she nursed Polly, they slept in the wagon; despite being dirt poor, they had still arrived as prepared as one could be. Yet *everything* had to be done. She and John looked at each other, nodded, and then walked away. They knew they had to get to work.

Hours passed. Luraney took her large apple basket and baby and roamed around the general area, looking for food, more apples, other fruit, and nuts and berries especially. Well, what *would be* fruits and nuts and berries ...once spring and summer's end came. Too late now; still, Luraney, who was schooled in the practical and land-dependent rural life of Tennessee, recognized the plants themselves. Luckily, she found them in abundance. Butternut walnut -*some call them*

15

white walnuts, she recalled. *Oh, I see up there are some deerberry, elderberry, what I believe are strawberry plants even.*

She let out a breath. *These slopes can sure get steep* ...she stopped for a moment, wishing for a drink. Time to head back down; find a creek to coat her thirst. Pregnant or not, her basket, her Polly, and her belly had to keep moving.

Oh, and John's favorite, she thought as she walked along; hadn't realized she'd climbed to such higher elevations *-blackberries. He will be happy.* But they attract bears, and she told herself to file away the blackberry patch's location.

She had to hold herself, her daughter, and her basket back as she stamped down the mountain, the slope so steep, she had to really concentrate not to lose control and spin right down the mountain. When she finally reached the creek, she sat for some nice long sips, closing her eyes. *Thank you, Lord.* She was incredibly grateful to God for providing so quickly. Opening her eyes, she eyed the creek as it swam itself downstream, over rocks and bigger rocks, and with logs freshly fallen, clogging its way. A reminder of the dangers that can occur at any time.

Quenched for now, Luraney rose from the creekside and walked to their desired homestead, still a wild parcel of land. Seeing her husband, she stopped and watched him closely.

John had such energy today—she could see it in his eyes—and was making a thorough reconnaissance of the area. She could read his mind: where would he plant his crops? He crouched down and fingered the soil, rich, not crumbly at all, nice and black. *Oh yes,* he thought. Yes. He was happy. He stood and looked around. Definitely, this is home. He knew it, felt it in his bones. *Finally, I am master of my own land. I have a farm. I am somebody.*

The rest of that first day passed in a flash of activity. Finding a place for her food stash. Gathering more wood for a cooking fire. Luraney glanced up at the mountains, the sun just dipping below its peaks. Colors came out, painting the light with pink, orange and red. She breathed deeply, noticing Polly stir in the sling. *Had she really been in the sling all day? Goodness, if today is any indication, time will certainly get away from us. We'll have to be as efficient with time as possible. So much to do....*

The young mother's basket was filled and she knew she would be busy drying, canning and preserving the fresh food in the coming days and weeks—once they were settled. Once they had a house. Thank goodness the cool air would preserve the apples for now. She wished it were early summer and wondered again about their decision to come to the cove now, in late, late fall. Still lots of reservations about this move. *Well, we didn't know what to expect and Joshua Jobe told us that any time, any season, would be just perfect.* Hmmph! She walked and wondered. *Jobe said he'd be back in the morning ....*

With sudden clarity and realization, she knew. She just knew. *He wasn't moving here until next year. Until after the winter! He already knows and isn't telling us....*

Luraney met John just then, coming in from the fields. Good thing, for her mind was not at ease and she needed distraction. She made a humble dinner of dried deer meat and fresh apples. They never even started a fire that evening. Too tired. Settling back into the wagon, she nursed Polly, rubbed her small, but growing belly, and snuggled into her sleeping quilts for a long, deep sleep, knowing full well that the next day and the next and the next would be the hardest days she'd ever known. She was still nervous, but deep, deep down, something else, something new, was rising. *The beauty of this place ...it should compensate for any hardships ...I already love it here.*

Their first night was uneventful, punctuated by the deepest sleep the couple had ever known. The morning bloomed crisp and bright, laser beams of sunshine pointing the way, reassuring breezes hugging their spirits.

"Here!" John stated with conviction. "Right here will be our new home." He walked around the northeast corner of the cove at dawn, the drier portion, looking out to the basin of land that he would tame. Luraney agreed, walking behind him, Polly at her hip, wanting to keep her daughter close by until she'd learned the lay of the land. *This is a perfect place,* she thought. It would have to be cleared of trees, of course, but John could do it, they had a horse to help, and it was high enough to be dry, yet close enough to the creek, and seemed to be teeming with game. She looked around, and she and John finalizing their assessment grasped eyes and nodded their heads in harmony. Yes, this spot was tucked away and enfolded into the land. *Safe,* she thought. *Bountiful.*

They got to work.

John constructed a crude, but sufficient shelter for their first winter. He'd first cleared the land and cut down some trees. One room built of rough-hewn logs crisscrossed over one another, all standing on flat rocks for a foundation. One log at a time. About seven feet tall, because he was only one man and he could only lift the logs so high. But a quickly made wooden ladder could allow him to raise that roof later, even if on his own. Holes plugged with mud, no windows—at least for now—floors turned out a tad uneven, the fireplace that wasn't quite straight; yet the home was surprisingly well-built and would do until additions and improvements could be made. When time permitted, he already had plans to raise the height, add an upstairs loft and a porch with an angled roof.

But for now, it was a solid home base. The first one he could call his very own.

Luraney set her sights on finding some late corn that was likely spread or planted by the Indians, beating it into cornmeal from mortar and pestle—of course, there were no grist mills around—and no supplies coming down that primitive dirt road. *No, not a primitive dirt road—that was giving it too much credit. It was a trail that was barely recognizable. A gap in the woods,* she thought with a sigh. *And no supplies coming ...of course not! Jobe had known all along he'd not return so soon. Maybe not ever....*

She was very faithful—firmly believed God would get them through anything—but at times, the need for positivity failed her. She was human after all, and there was a quiet confidence that she knew who she was, and did not fret over who she ought to be. That trait of practicality, in the end, reassured her: *it's okay to feel the way I feel.*

Lucretia Oliver *did* feel it all—wondered and marveled and worried about her new home. It was certainly beautiful, this sub-range sliver of the Appalachians. *But those Indians ...this land was still their land.* At least, that's what the friendly, but intimidating red and brown, almost naked, men thought. Jobe had told them to come here and get land. For free. All they had to do was find a place and build. And it would be theirs. Free land. Jobe was a wealthy man, but also *very kind and liberal,* so *he should know as much as anyone about these things*, John kept repeating. Luraney sighed to herself. Nothing is free, she knew.

"It's definitely our right to be here since there's no land treaty, no land title, and by and by, Jobe knows all 'bout these things. He would never steer us wrong." John told Luraney yet again, when they spoke about it one night over a meager dinner cooked over the cabin's fireplace. It had been a few weeks now and they were comfortable. A quilt hung over the bed footboard that John had made, cooking utensils hung on wooden hooks plugged into the hearth, and cans were waiting to be filled with preserved winter food. The more settled they became, the more Luraney was always concerned about the Indians. She felt she was invading their home somehow, even if they didn't live here. They hunted here, gathered food, but it's true that they went somewhere else to live.

"I don't understand why they don't live here, John," she was anxiously saying. "It's so perfect. Where we are is dry and close to lots o' water ...the creek downright roars after a good rain. I sometimes wonder if they do live here and we just don't know it."

"Oh no. No. No, that's crazy talk. If they lived here, we'd have seen their houses. Or tents. Shelters." John was cleaning his flintlock Kentucky rifle, nicknamed Ol' Blue. It even had a decorative inlay, something he was very proud of. All men named their guns ...they knew it brought good luck. But he was listening closely to his wife; he'd heard the rising unease in her voice.

"Then, there's a reason they don't live here! It's too perfect. Why wouldn't they?"

"I don't know. But they *are* different from us, Luraney. They think and live differently." He used his nickname for her, trying to soothe her nerves. She narrowed her eyes at that; noticing her husband's attempts at softening and easing. She sighed audibly but tempered her tone.

"I still don't understand."

"And perhaps no one ever will." John caught his wife's skeptical eye. She wasn't one to dismiss a thought just like that. She stewed on things, just like the pot of rabbit meat over the fire. Had to understand the world around her. He would have to shift his talk.

"But we're here now. And it's a great new life!" John smiled and was suddenly so enthusiastic, holding Ol' Blue up to the fire to see its proudly polished gleam that Luraney couldn't bring herself to bring up any more of her many, many doubts. Yet, despite her practiced silence at the end of these fireside talks, Luraney never forgot that she and John were alone in a wilderness both perfect and inhumane. Their wagon had stopped after a long journey, at a plot of land tucked back into the tall trees, with promising cropland all around and a view of the old mountains to always remind them of the dangers of the thick brush, Indians, and the winter that had arrived. *As if we needed reminding,* she thought. But they were here now. And the young Oliver family had taken Jobe at his word and once arrived, proceeded to stake a claim to their very own land in the cove.

Another morning dawned and Joshua Jobe did not show up.

Nor the next, nor the next.

It had been many weeks now.

"Lucretia. It's big! And it's ours. There's no one else in sight. Not for miles. Maybe longer. It's all ours. Save for a couple Indians roamin' about. But they won't bother us. Look here, they haven't bothered us so far! There's a place in the upper end of this here cove, see?" He pointed his finger towards the northwest. "Let's go. See what this place offers up." Every day dawned bright during those early, isolated days, and John's enthusiasm was contagious. He'd finally realized his dream! It was like he was a new man. At long last, he now owned his own farm, was building it, preparing and working it, raising his family ...exploring every corner of this new world of his. A man's pinnacle of success. Imagine what that does to the spirit! Why, it makes it fly up to the rooftops of heaven.

As they inspected their land more and more, learned the landmarks and creeks, they became much more comfortable in this new land. Large boulders and that largest and broadest of chestnut trees over to the west stood guard. Still, almost every morning, Luraney woke with anticipation, while also harboring secret deep reservations, and some mornings, the secret got the best of her. Oh, how she fought it! But those icy dawns greeting her as she began her day's work, looking up at her first crude home, it was all she could do to not head out right this very moment to the more populated and comfortable parts of Tennessee. Where she grew up. Oh, no, it wasn't ideal. She'd been poor ...abandoned even! *A bound girl.* And her marriage ...to a good loving man, but they'd been so incredibly poor too. So, why did she long for those days? *Perhaps because I knew what to expect. Even if it was expecting nothing. Here, it's all unknown.*

What future did they truly have here?

At this very moment, on one of those early mornings shrouded in such mist that she barely saw the peaks towering above, on a day where she woke up with knots of trepidation, she just couldn't see it. *We are not designed to be hunter-gatherers! I want Polly to have nicer things, an easier life ...and the new baby ...what kind of life will we have? Maybe John would've made it as a collier for a while. Then, he'd have done something else. Maybe. Set aside a little money... What if we die here? All of us? Will our children be taken by Indians? Wolves? Will we get through this winter?*

John came walking up the path from the field just then, enthusiastic as ever. His walk was jaunty and he was as happy as if he had any good sense at all. And just as he arrived, no doubt to relay what wonderful sights he had just seen, Luraney erupted—a rarity—and voiced all her fears of the past, present and future to her husband.

He stood stock-still for a moment, numbed by this sudden torrent from his wife. *What was this crackup?* He looked around. No one. Nothing amiss. No sign of an accident, an errant animal or burned food. No Indians—he'd have seen them. Polly was laying on a blanket close by, happily playing with her toes.

But of course, he knew his wife. And he knew of her fears and character—the need to worry it all out of the system. John did the only thing a man could do in such a situation.

He sat down in the spirit of compromise and looked directly into her eyes. He listened.

For a long time, she emptied her worries. Still, he listened.

"But Lucretia!" he finally ventured, in defiant desperation, after letting her go on the rant for minutes upon full minutes. "This is my only chance to own my own land. You *know* this!" His own emotions threatened to erupt if he wasn't careful. They couldn't afford to both crack up at the same time. He toggled his tone of voice down a notch or two. Stood up and began pacing.

"And we're doing better. Remember my soldiering? I was afraid ...of everyone! Everything! Why? More so of the fact that I never had a chance at anythin' in life! I was afraid that my life would fall flat with no success.

But Jackson showed me...."

"Andrew Jackson! I know all about Jackson." She said with spitting bitterness. "You hero worship him too much! He's filled your head with too-grand ideas. Just because you men beat the entire Creek Nation in a short period of time don't mean that will happen all the time." Lucretia could tell he wasn't listening to truly hear her by now; simply was silent to let it get out of her system.

"Everything since has been heading upwind! We got married. Polly was born on July 18, 1817, Lucretia. Well after any threat. And General Jackson gained all that land for us...." He heard her sigh. He continued but immediately switched his thought to another vein, hearing the bubbling rise again. "There was enough supplies, we did it. I know you were worried, but we made it. We were leaders. Jackson. Every soldier. Including *me*. Because he allowed us to be masters of our own fates. "Think for yourselves," he'd say. "Follow orders yes, but use some sense in the meantime!" "But that's beside the point. It ain't about the war. Or Jackson. It's about our chances here in the cove. No need to be scared ...look! We're fine! And soon, we will have company."

"What company? Jobe hasn't returned! And he probably never will!" she spewed bitterly. "He lied, John!" Oh, she was trying. Truly she was. But she could not keep the fear, and the fast-growing sharp hostility from her tone, and it erupted with fury.

He walked away from his wife, wanting to be compassionate, wanting to compromise, but he was never going to let this one chance at success get away. He had just told her so and had repeated it for so long now. And for her part, she didn't say another word. Stewing for a few minutes, the couple, with no one else around, was silent. They watched Polly gathering sticks by the creek, laughing at a squirrel. Luraney huffed a dispirited laugh, wishing life was simple again. Just then, the eagle soared over and landed on a stout tree limb jutting right over their cabin. Peering at the man who had found his home, it saw his eyes. Ruffling its feathers, it let out a loud squawk and flew westward. John stopped pacing, watched the bird fly over to the largest and broadest of chestnut trees, devoid of all leaves now. He turned around and looked at his wife dead in the eyes. "This is my chance. The only one. I will take it or I will die."

He said it just loud enough for Lucretia to hear and for her boldness to lie down and think for a moment. She was laser-focused on just surviving, and the approaching bitter cold of deeper winter, and her daughter, her husband, and food, and her pregnancy, Indians ...just surviving.

He walked back over to her. "Just look, Luraney." He took her shoulders and gently spun her around towards the valley. There they were. The most beautiful of mountains, looking as if the earth was wearing an endless skirt of soft pleats as the afternoon shadows waved their breezes through towering trees. He then kissed her neck and embraced her—a rarity for such men. Affection only when it was required. With tears in her eyes, she allowed herself to be turned around and looked out at the cove. Took a breath. And another. He's right. She was here now. *Bloom where you are planted.* She closed her eyes, breathed, opened them, looked again; tried looking with fresh, tearful eyes. John continued to have his hands on her shoulders, sometimes gripping them tightly, reassuringly. She could feel his breath in her hair.

And soon, perhaps for the first time, she felt her feet on the ground stand still. Not itching to run or climb up a ladder to a wagon to escape. Not pointing to the road out. *I am here now.* Her inner sensations stopped fighting and tugging. She sucked in her breath at the sight of the bird. For the eagle returned, soared overhead just then, letting out a squawk of satisfaction. She looked up; saw a large stick in its beak. *Building a nest. One stick at a time.* So peaceful! She then

25

caught a glimpse of a lone deer. A buck with a magnificent velvety rack. Graceful in its movements, it looked straight at the human woman, blinked, and dropped its head to graze again. *He is not afraid at all. And, that eagle ...one stick at a time ...it will take him forever to build his home...and in the thick of winter ...* She laughed just then and felt her anxiety break. *Perhaps we are not so alone after all.* With flowing tears, but also a half-formed smile, she turned to her husband and kissed him back, realizing she would have to find a way, one stick at a time.

Between their little Polly, and her progressing pregnancy, finding game, gathering remnants of late berries, fruits and nuts, shoring up the cabin, and making sure they had enough wood for fuel and warmth, John and Lucretia Oliver kept busy preparing for their first winter in the cove, already here, but fast accelerating. It certainly helps the soul's battlefield to keep busy. Keeps the worrisome thoughts from overwhelming. The couple was as industrious as they could be. But when the big change of season came with a vicious and icy snowfall, all of their preparation was no match for the brutality of an awakening glacial winter.

"My God, we are starving!" She cried. "And there's no one around! No one to help us!"

She cried tears of frustration and fear. "No one even knows we are here! What a wasteland!"

"Lucretia," John demanded, using her given name, realizing that her practicality was not winning over her fear at this moment. She had been doing well lately, but now, he knew what he had to do. He had to keep her calm. Talk her off the ledge to a cooler head. There was no room for such distress; they must rely on their fortitude ...and each other.

26

"We are *not* here alone. We have each other. There are Indians who haven't bothered us none. Jobe will be back in the spring. And there ain't nothin' we can do! We are here. We need to survive. And that's *that*." Always pragmatic, the only white man of the cove, responsible for his little growing family, John couldn't afford to show fear. Or break down. Neither could Luraney, though she was clearly breaking down. Cracking. They *were* literally starving. Just like when he was a collier. Damn. It was all supposed to be better. Harder maybe, but better. *My own land.* Instead, it was worse. And now with a baby! With one on the way! How would they survive?

Bleakness descended upon the chilly little cabin of the tiny cove family. Nothing moved in the snowy, white, barren landscape. The anguish and hunger extended from the family to the land. Nothing moved. Nothing grew. The occasional small deer or white rabbit or even a small squirrel kept the family alive, but barely. For a lone squirrel couldn't provide enough meat for a stew with nothing else in it. They hadn't had time or opportunity to put potatoes, corn, carrots, or other such sustenance away for the winter. A few chestnuts, some apples whose supply was now severely dwindled, and other such food were all that was left. Luraney would sit in her chair by the window, rocking her fussy baby, rubbing her small belly—smaller than it should've been—and prayed with her hand on her Bible. She couldn't read very well, but she knew what was in The Book. It gave her at least some comfort, thinking that the words would bleed into her struggling soul. It was all she could do.

John went outside of the little cabin and made his way across the woods, tracking and stalking any animal he could find. The cold was brutal, but he kept moving. The eagle swooped overhead, the first time he'd seen the bird in weeks. He smiled to himself upon seeing the familiar creature. Up ahead, he saw movement. He stopped and watched; as they came into view, he realized there were a few Cherokees walking towards their place. *Where were they going? Were they out hunting too?* He looked at his cabin, trying to determine what to do. They'd been friendly thus far, but of course he'd heard stories... He glanced back towards the cabin, the smoke coming out of their homestead, smelled the weak, gamey aroma of something that poor Luraney was trying to cook; he saw the fence posts he'd been laying aside to enclose their garden once the snows thawed and spring came and glanced at his axe leaning against the tree. *I need to build a place for the barn, corncrib, a tool place ...a garden enclosure, animal pens ...if we ever get animals besides the horse...no, we'd never eat our horse,* although they would admit they'd thought of it. More often than they'd like to admit. *Are we even safe here?* He wished his axe was closer, but, like any self-sufficient man, he had his trusty rifle, Ol' Blue, and now, he held it tight. *So much to do. What do they want with us?*

Lost in thought, chest-thumping, John snapped back when he noticed that the Cherokees were moving closer, directly towards him, and they had something in their hands. Clearly, they were coming to his home. There were about twelve of them. Spears in some hands, other hands holding something bulky in a colorful parfleche. The Indians stopped when they saw John, hesitated a moment, then continued their walk up to the white man. They knew each other of course, by sight anyway, but they'd had little true interaction. The Cherokee had discussed the white man, but they figured one little family wouldn't cause them any harm. In fact, they felt sorry for the pioneers, for they were clearly struggling.

The leader approached, dressed in heavy buckskin for warmth and holding a parfleche, held his hands palm side up and spoke.

"Ostu iga," the leader said with a smile. They did not appear in the least threatening and John took a breath, and loosened his grip on his rifle.

"Good day to you too." John nodded. He did not speak Cherokee, nor did the Indians speak the white man's language. Yet both groups managed to pick up a few words here and there, ones of greeting, and to help with basic trade communication.

John smiled at them. "I am glad to see you." He lowered his gun.

The Cherokee looked at one another and the leader nodded his head to the others. John felt momentary panic when the Indian handed over the parfleche. John held out his hand to take it but did not open it up.

"Open." The large Cherokee stepped forward, opened the parfleche and held it open to the white man.

"Agisdi. Eat."

John couldn't believe it. There was food inside. The Indians were helping them! They were helping his family!

"Adolonige."

"Dried orange?" He felt he understood most of what they were saying. But he saw the Indians exchange puzzled glances.

John tried again. "Pumpkin?"

"W!" It sounded like Un-Une.

Lone man and Indian group smiled at each other. One had mist in his eyes when he looked back at his meager homestead, wife on the front porch looking terrified.

"Luraney! Come meet the Cherokee! They are giving us food!"

After doing a stumblingly decent job communicating with each other, John and Luraney invited the Cherokee Indians into their home to warm up—which they accepted, and to eat—which they declined. They warmed their hands by the fire and looked around, just like anyone would do when invited into another's habitat. They patted Polly's head and said words that the two pioneers couldn't quite catch. But they only stayed long enough to warm up, all the while smiling and bowing gratefully. The two groups—the twelve Cherokee Indians and the three-person pioneer family tried to talk to one another as best they could and soon said their farewells.

John put his hands together as if in prayer and said a heartfelt "Wado," one of the words he knew. He then extended his hand to the leader.

The Cherokee—each and every one—took his hand, and replied, "You are very welcome," before walking out of the warm cabin and off to their winter home. Where it was located was a mystery to the pioneers. But for now, that generous portion of dried pumpkin, haunch of bear meat, and a bundle of dried fruits would make for a life-changing feast for the coming days. And it would not be the only encounter with their unexpected life support group. For whatever reason—perhaps just pure humanity—the Cherokees paid the small family a few more visits throughout the winter, each time bringing food. They usually came right after an especially icy storm.

Humanity excels at making generalities -*I hate them! I don't want them here! That's their problem, not mine! They are not like us*... but when it came down to face to face, eye to eye or close contact, few could refuse the softening of their hearts towards sufferers and most, in turn, gratefully reached out to the extended foreign hand. And so it was. The Indians brought the poor, starving white family simple, but no less than life-saving, gifts. Many people move the world, yet make no thunder.

That first winter was frosty and cold, and very snowy, yet the young couple could still see the great potential of the land and prayed every day for spring and better times. Luraney's grit and resolve solidified, and she sewed quilts, played with Polly, and kept the fire going. Thank goodness they had enough wood stockpiled. John managed to shoot some game throughout the arctic season to see them through. He would always offer food to the Indians when they arrived, and they always refused politely. Luraney no longer felt any fear of the Indians. In fact, she welcomingly searched for them coming from the West, trusting that they just wanted to help. It was an eye-opening and humbling experience to understand so very different people; ones who were once feared, but who proved to be true friends.

Cades Cove, in the winter of 1818-1819 saw a population of three—John, Luraney, and Polly. Of course, there were the Indians and scarce others around the general area, but the fertile valley bowl itself was nearly empty. A household of two adults and one small child was not exactly what the pioneers had in mind. Luckily, life isn't stagnant, and seasons, as well as circumstances, change. As the winter snows melted, and the ancient earth tilted her icy face towards her great shining star, the creeks filled with thawing snow, budding trees and plants were well-watered, and the now abundant springtime game bounded in plain view. Spring stirred slowly at first, then throwing off her white quilted covers, the secluded cove showed a bit more of what the original settlers were striving and hoping for. Leaves, blooms, stirrings in the forest, young fawns and cubs, water rushing, flowers, bees, crisp air with hints of warmth ...all of this lushness dressed the valley in its finest attire. *We learned. We survived.* Worries thawed and hope flowed. And, because they managed to survive, the Olivers would never be alone again.

ᘓᕫᕢ Chapter Two ᘓᕫᕢ

SPRING 1819- JOBE COMES BACK

"Jobe is back!" John cried as he rushed across the fields to his nestled home. "Jobe! It's Jobe!" He had managed to plant the staples: corn, oats, wheat, rye, and various vegetables; had planted their kitchen garden with Luraney, enclosed their homestead with fencing, and otherwise created a much better hub of sustenance for his family. Their chances were now much, much better. Still, life was hard. "There were no mills around, so they had to beat their grain by hand, in mortise—a kind of mortar and pestle using a hole cut into wood, using the finer part for bread and the coarser for hominy." Luraney's arms were very strong in no time at all, and the exertion was normally very healthy, but all that strain exhausted her with each passing day.

Luraney, now well along in her pregnancy, heard the commotion and her husband's yells that morning, and soon heard for herself the wagon wheels, more hollering; hurrying as much as she could down the porch steps and outside the house to look. Polly squealed with joy at the sight of horses and people, having been right outside the home cleaning the stone and gravel walkway to the home. She heard her father's shouts and stood up on solid little legs.

"I's picking weeds," she proudly exclaimed to her mother, showing fistfuls of grass and sticks. "Yes, Polly. You are pickin' weeds. Cleaning the walkway is called pickin' at the weeds." Despite the rustic and rugged environment, John and Luraney's constant and prideful attention made for a neat and tidy homestead, and children learned as early as possible to contribute.

As the couple watched the approaching crowd, they were astonished to see that Joshua Jobe did not come alone. He led a wagon train of others, seemingly packed with provisions and healthy hands. "Jobe is back! And we have neighbors! My goodness, he's brought a crowd." Luraney cried, shocked and overjoyed to the point of tears, forgetting for a moment her anger at him for leaving them alone last winter.

John was now at her side, amazed at the sight. He, too, was visibly moved as they watched the approaching progress of men, women and even a few children. He wiped his forehead and eyes with his ragged kerchief.

"It ain't just people they're brinin' Luraney. You know they'll have brought goods. Tools."

"Mmm hmmm ..." Luraney murmured, still staring, not quite believing the luck that was arriving today. "Probably have some seeds and some cloth. Skillets? If they have an extra, I sure could swap for one. John, if you help them with their houses, and gather some firewood, we may get another skillet. Of course, they'd also be bringin' their most important of possessions—their family Bibles. Sure'd be nice to have others to pray with."

Everything one would need for a new life in the mountains was packed into the wagon train. Certainly, goods, tools, seeds, and a new skillet would be welcomed. But beyond material items, however necessary they were, these new inhabitants swinging the rickety dance as they rode in their wagons, would bring assistance, friendship, and family ties. Luraney thought of options opening up for neighborly exchanges of pies and quilts. Of meeting by the fence for tea or coffee. Of children growing up together. Of Polly's courtship and marriage—when the time came of course. Of praying together. The closer the group got, the more John, Luraney and even little Polly Oliver felt a quickening inside and they all realized that they were witnessing something very profound. John was the one who actually said it out loud: "Look at that. We are witnessing the very birth of the Cades Cove Community." They stood in silence, in awe actually, as the crowd grew closer and closer. Rare is a time when one views an actual miracle.

"Yes," he continued, turning to Luraney who was just about to say something along the same lines to her husband. They smiled at one another, so close they read each other's thoughts.

"Cades Cove. You've heard the stories ...the Indian Chief's wife, Kate. Jobe couldn't remember the whole story, or maybe he could and didn't want to talk about the Indians and scare you off...but I do believe it was dubbed Kate's Cove. Now, we shall call it Cades Cove. Officially. Always. No more back and forth and not rememberin' the name."

Luraney looked upwards, watching the eagle appear and begin circling the group, still not believing their luck and God's graces. The bird danced in the wind, joyfully diving down and up again. When he caught the wind, he stretched his wings to their full extent.

"Our home," John Oliver said formally and solemnly, "now has a name."

Jobe's group and the Olivers greeted one another warmly, but the newly arrived did not stay long that first day. They needed to stake out a place for their own homesteads before sundown. "The great thing is," Jobe told the group, sweeping his hand across the scenery as they disbursed, "was like I said...you can take whatever land you wanna. Pick the best tract and go wit' it." Further talk, formal meetings, and catching up would have to wait. Life never stood still even when embraced in the mountains' arms. But that night, Luraney went to bed early, warmed by a roaring fire and plenty of food, and slept better than she had since arriving in the cove.

A few days went by, *enough time for him to get settled in. But not enough time to let my chances go by.* Joshua Jobe was barely settled into the cove when Luraney paid him a visit, bent on telling Mr. Jobe just what she thought of him for persuading them to move to the cove. *And lying about coming back! No sir ...I know I should show some mercy and forgiveness, but what he done to me and John—not to mention Polly, a child!—was unforgivable.* Luraney was angry that they had truly almost died; they starved a lot of long nights, any hope of escape and returning to other parts of Tennessee made impossible by icy roads and too-harsh conditions. That and her husband's refusal to leave, of course. *I'll make it here or die tryin.' You could no sooner move that biggest of chestnut trees than move me outta this cove!* But Jobe didn't have to know that.

Her sweet baby girl had suffered, and all this during her second pregnancy too! The Indians ...though they turned out to be friendly ...*but we didn't know that at first! They could've killed us right there in the little cabin, and smeared pumpkin on our scalps ...You promised you'd be back in the morning....*

36

She marched across the cove to the Jobe homestead, where he had erected a crude cabin over the past few days. She saw he was now busy with fencing, and mapping out his crops.

"Mr. Jobe. Nice to see you here." She spoke in a sharp, clipped voice, looked him straight in the eye, and then took a deep breath. "But let me tell you..." Hands on hips, her tone told him she was dead serious, and none too happy.

Jobe smiled at the spunky young lady, about to spit fire at him. "How are you getting along in this new country, Lucretia?" "We hadn't a chance to catch up right yet...only just arrived ..."

"I *know* you just arrived!" she interrupted. "And, I am starving to death, sir!"

Realizing these *were* her new neighbors and God was always watching, she tried reigning herself in, chest rising, moved her hands higher on the hips. Alright, perhaps she wasn't starving right now, but she *had been* starving, for many nights and days, and while pregnant! And her little Polly had cried for food many, many times. So pitifully by many a fire, her mother's tears reflected in Ol' Blue's gleaming barrel. And she told Jobe all of that, right now, in the nicest of no uncertain terms.

Jobe's smile faded as Lucretia Oliver continued to let him know, loudly, that they were thinking about leaving the cove. Blamed him. Accused him of lying. He didn't know what the big deal was. The Oliver family was lucky! They'd had their pick of the cove's great land and the choicest site for their home ...they made friends with the Indians, they had food...they'd survived. And now, look at those crops. Why, there's gonna be plenty of food! John was a strong man. Capable. He'd done a lot; more than Jobe thought any man on his own could do. In fact, he'd been extremely impressed with the state of the Oliver homestead and lamented not coming back sooner. Yes, John Oliver was a strong man. But Luraney, he was finding out, was even stronger.

Looking around, he couldn't understand how anyone would want to leave this stunning place, with the most beautiful scenery, fertile land, game all around. Of course, *he* had left, but that was with full intentions of coming back quickly. How was he to know it wouldn't be until the next spring? That unexpected business would keep him with plans delayed through the winter?

Turning back to Luraney Oliver, he could see that she was very, very cross. And he immediately knew what he needed to do to convince her to stay. They needed John's experience with the soil, the game, the weather. The Indians... And Luraney's experience was of utmost importance for that matter. For the Olivers were the only two of their people who had ever survived a Cades Cove winter.

"Why is it so important to you that we stay? *You* can stay if you wish. Why us?"

She noticed that he didn't answer.

"Lucretia." He used her given name to show her how serious he was. "My brother is coming in a few weeks to the cove. He's bringing a herd of milk cows. Please stay. You have neighbors now. And if you stay ..." he sighed, knowing what he had to do to appease her. "If you stay, I will give you a choice of two cows."

He continued, honeying his tongue. "Please...I will give you the very best cows—you choose. You will be ...no, *we* will be fine with them here. Milk, cheese, butter. It will get better." Lucretia's bones told her to deny this gift, deny his kind talk, to go home to Carter County in the northeast corner of Tennessee. After a considerable cease-fire, her soul was, again, waging a battle between the cove finally feeling like home, versus still having reservations and wanting a permanent retreat. Oh, she didn't really mean they were seriously thinking of leaving because she knew they wouldn't actually go—probably ever, and she didn't really want to go now that she was used to it. And of course, John would never leave ...and she'd never leave him. But Luraney wanted to get back at Jobe, to make him realize the situation he led them to and left them with. She was usually forgiving and mannerly - *of pretty easy character,* her childhood volunteer family had said of her—but with such highly charged situations as fearful starvation and fighting for her family's safety, as well as with characters like Jobe, the need to be tough and resolute flared up with full force.

"After all, why would life get better with milk, butter and cheese?" Her tone was strong, still taking stabs at her husband's friend. And suddenly, she felt like crying, the battle rising within. "You fussin' about all this country charm here in these mountains. But it's hard work! We need a lot more than that to make this place better!" Jobe saw her balking and discouragement and simply kept talking, touting the benefits of two cows and neighbors.

"Can you differentiate between these two benefits, if you please? Cows and people?" she said tartly, directing her sour tone at him.

Whoa, my work is cut out for me here. But if he just kept talking ...she may forgive him. It was the only thing he could do. "We've a chance to make our own community! *You* two started it. The Olivers. How many people in history get that chance?"

"John," she told her husband that night with a deep sigh, "He talked so good and kind that I could say no more." They were sitting around their fire inside the cabin, made more comfortable with abundant food stored away, their daughter sleeping in a bed in the loft and one more warm quilt Luraney was able to complete. She planned it for the new baby, due around July—a few more months, if she had her timing right. Which she probably didn't, being so early on when they'd arrived. No matter. *Babies have their own timetable.* It was late in the evening, and the couple was tired. Life on the land forced early bedtimes and early rises, but tonight was a bit different. The couple needed to catch up, talk it out.

"Luraney." He said, taking her hands warmed by the fire. "You're a real good woman. Thank you for believing in me and this new life. I promise. Things'll get better. They already are, you got to admit...." She sighed again, but this time, contentedly; kissed her husband back. And then smiled at her kind, strong John. The one who was simply following his dreams; toiling away to make *her* life better too.

She thought back to her conversation with Joshua Jobe earlier. "It did me good, that talk."

"I see it did."

"John, I just had'a release all my anxieties, my thoughts, my anger."

"I know." He took her hand, kissed it, and went to lay down on the bed.

"I'll be in bed shortly."

First though, Luraney had to think on things just a bit more. Marinating in thought, her mind slipped back to when she and John had come to the cove. *1818 thereabouts. Thereabouts ...ha! How could she forget? Of course she knew the year, the month, even the hour of the day! It was just a few months ago! But it felt like ages since she'd left her corner of Tennessee with her husband, the soldier veteran of the War of 1812, the poor collier whose dream was "to own my own farm one day," He'd said it to her quite often, and hadn't she always known he would? He was just that type of man. Enlisted into the Army at Knoxville on January 5, 1814—the War of 1812 still raging—into Captain Adam Winsell's Company, Colonel Ewen Allison's Regiment, East Tennessee Militia. He was a responsible, honorable man, but had grown up poor—he always talked about how poor he was—during their early courtship. Courtship being what it was in those days.*

They'd arrived here with barely a thing. A vast wilderness with many immediate hardships, loneliness, penetrating fear. But, she admitted to herself, there was something magical about this cove, nestled deep in the bosom of the mountains. John and I—we threw our hands up in the air and released our deepest desires; we did not know what God would catch and toss back down. He made us suffer, learn....appreciate.

John had cleared fields at the lower end of the cove, a swamp in actuality. But their house was high and dry. The first priority for any new settler was to make a shelter and plant crops. Mess up these priorities and the rest wouldn't matter for they'd be dead as soon as humanly possible. Nature would be sure of that.

Indians were spotted, but then, they'd turn out to be saviors. Who would'a thought?

Then, when the rains came, He released back to us the dreams we threw up to heaven. God had tossed back such lush and rich scenes; they left permanent imprints on the heart.

I wouldn't leave now even if I could. This is my home.

Luraney got up from her chair and put one more log into the fire. She was tired, but not ready for bed yet. John, she saw as she glanced over to the bed, was already asleep; Polly—that sweet blessing—long asleep. She was still alone with her thoughts, where she preferred them to be, nice and close by, keeping her company tonight. Thoughts tortured her many a night, but tonight's stirrings brought a hugging comfort. Luraney's curse and comfort was that her mind ran through countless fields, and she remembered everything.

Luraney took her hair out of her bun and shook it out. Running her fingers through her soft brown hair, she sat back down, shifted in her chair, causing John to stir in his sleep. He wasn't the reflective type; too busy achieving his dreams. Luraney, on the other hand, needed to sit and marinate in her thoughts until they were worked out completely. She *had* to work it out. You know what she means by that. She needs to sit, think, and get through the stages of anger, from stewing, to planning, to accepting this crossing of her life. Toggling between gratefulness and that hugging comfortable feeling, to the niggling anxieties and doubtfulness that creeps in immediately afterward.

Oh, why can't I just stick with one feeling? Yet, it was just this process that made the strongest of women.

For indeed, her life crossed over to something completely different than what she thought or planned. *Would her crossing—Oliver's Crossing—be successful. Happy? The smell of the fire was always present. As was the smell of animals, cooking, the creek, and the land …She'd been Lucretia Frazier, born of English parents, knowing a bit about her father, but not her mother, from a foster family, outspoken when called for—which was a nice, if a somewhat difficult foil to John's shyness. She'd married John in 1814, during the spring month of April. It was now spring of 1819. She had a daughter and another child on the way. And John was a good man. A good husband.* She smiled wryly at the never-ending narrative of her own life. She then laughed at herself ...at the toggled moment; both hardship and magic were melted together with the smell of the fire, the spirits of the two sleeping souls in the small log cabin, and the beautiful solace of mountain life. She rose from her chair. The switching between her gratefulness and practicality tugged at one another until her true self emerged the winner. It always did. She got up and slipped into bed, shifted right up against John's warm back. *I do love it here.* Closing her eyes, the narrative ended for the night. *But now, all I can think about is that I have two cows to look forward to.*

Exactly two weeks later Joshua, Jobe and his brother showed up at the Oliver homestead across from their own homestead. True to his word, he let Luraney choose the best two cows of the bunch.

"Let me say it ag'in ...reiterate." he said slowly, for effect, hanging on to the ropes and leading the cows. "These here are gifts. Free. I am glad you both are here. Truly." He told John and Luraney, and little Polly whose hair he ruffled. "She's a pretty, sweet little thing." He smiled at the child. "You know the more people in the cove, the better. Allow a lot of opportunities for futures." John and Luraney knew what he meant and wholeheartedly agreed. People grew up fast in the mountains, and neighbors and a community would mean family ties, marriages, more children and higher populations—all the things that ran through their heads when they first set eyes on Jobe's wagon train, returning late -*very late,* but better than never. Indeed, more people meant more opportunity to survive and prosper.

"The future." Luraney almost laughed, her continued wariness of Jobe sometimes still threatening her spirit, but that word *future* was showing very hopeful signs, much more often. She stood, looking at the two chosen cows, then walked away towards John, who was now walking around the corncrib, wondering where to put the cows. He'd started a barn, of course, for the horse, but he hadn't planned on two cows. At least not yet.

They needed a bigger, or a new, barn. A cantilevered barn would work best. A type of barn that had a counterweighted overhanging beam design originating in Europe. Upper loft is bigger than the base. That upper's for storin' hay, the cows and horse down below with plenty of room and air flows nicely through. See here, he grabbed a stick and drew the design in the dirt to show Luraney. A smaller box-like structure, with a bigger one right on top, with a large sloping roof. *When it rains, or snows, and when it gets too hot, the overhead level hangs over and shades them. Really keeps 'em warm and dry.* She had to admit, it made perfect sense.

They also needed feed for the cows. Or did they? Their fields produced and there was grass and hay everywhere. Would they need feed? Wouldn't the land provide? But these new neighbors sure were clearing a lot of room for fields. And they had brought a lot of animals ...Would there be enough?

Ugh, she thought, *why do I worry about every little thing?* Her feelings still wavered on a daily basis between steady gratefulness; sometimes despair, but most often, acceptance. Reality and practicality simply settled in to nest. *We live in the cove. Surrounded by mountains.* They were a long way from home—at least, the home that she knew. With lots of other people around lately, not just a few. They had started this community of Cades Cove. They lived there. And that was that.

Would the Oliver family just cross here? Would they stay? She really wanted to remain here if she was honest with most areas of her heart. In the other, smaller areas, and on darker days, she still wanted to flee with the cold wind that blew through the mountain bowl at her back. Lucretia honestly did not know how to feel right now. Mixed emotions, even if they leaned heavily towards the peaceful cove, are never easy to deal with. One must crouch behind the stone wall of the trench, enduring the pushing and pulling of war, the war won only when the fight ended, or one died. Morbidly sensitive, intelligent, a thinker, Luraney's soul remained a reluctant battlefield; on one side excitement, opportunity, resilience, patience, and honor. On the other, a strong sense of apprehension, injustice, and uneasy agitation.

Well, she thought, the afternoon gone and the battles having subsided for the day, *if death is invited to the show, it will be the last to leave if I can help it!* And with that lifelong, steely resolve, Luraney remained at the small barn, where the horse was munching on a pile of hay and began petting her two cows.

They were warm, content. Their smell was earthy, their breath sweet. Leathery skin, healthy and dry. Shedding her last gentle tears a few moments before—unseen to anyone whom she would've encountered—Luraney felt a sudden release standing here between her two cows. For perhaps the first time since arriving at this beautiful, isolated, swampy place, with barely a road and no other white men around, Indians lurking in every shadow (even if they did save her life), animals, hard work, she felt firmly settled. Determined even.

And so, it was then, right then, standing with the horse and two cows, no longer crouched behind the stone wall of an inner war, that she realized that the cows could enlarge her world.

I am married, we live in this cove, have a family, need to bloom where planted, and by Job—Jobe?—She laughed at the irony—I'd just better make the best of it. Stop this tug of war! She put her hands up to her temples, closed her eyes and gave a low sighing moan. *Stop this!* She admonished herself. A philosophical person always knows when the time comes to stop pulling. She opened her eyes and let loose the rope that was tugging her along.

Luraney perched on a low three-legged stool that John had crafted, resting her chin on her hands. Such paraphernalia in a barn! They really were outgrowing it. Piles of hay ...over there was the hardened saddle hanging on a large wooden peg securely plugged between slats, reins hanging down, a metal bit. They all mixed together with a packed earthen floor in a smell of warm recognition. She inhaled deeply the aroma of dung and dry, sturdy fur. Somehow, right there in the barn that was really only big enough for just the one horse, the two cows, the fertile potential of the land and the sheer magical beauty of the site engulfed her, at least enough to set her resolve and make up her mind once and for all. At least for today. *No, not for today. Today. And every day.*

"I will make soap." she said to herself, remembering the steps needed. This simple decision was the equivalent of snapping her fingers and there appearing a fully stocked general store, twenty cows, sacks of good coffee, and glass windows. For this practical act was to be the start of Luraney's blooming within the cove, as well as starting valuable community resources.

It was the first time in recorded history that soap was made in this particular bowl of the mountains. Soap was made with lye, ashes, tallow, lard, and milk. *Funny how different animals' fat makes for different feels. Bear fat makes for a thick and meaty soap. So does beef. Others make for softer soap, a nicer texture.*

She mixed the ingredients together and heated them up. Then, the cooling process; all that water had to evaporate, which actually took longer than she'd anticipated. Some early bars were just too crumbly. Or didn't lather at all. Felt like holding a rough and scaly bear paw. Some had a God-awful smell that she threw right back into the fire. But Luraney was a quick study, never making the same mistakes twice, and to her surprise, discovered that she had creativity. Crushed walnuts and honey could also be added, and Luraney added the best she could find to her products. Experimenting, she found, was enjoyable and had purpose. *The cows really did expand my world.* She laughed at that thought. Luraney Oliver's soap was soon much coveted by her family and neighbors.

"It's the little things," she said to her little family one evening, weeks later, when she had all but perfected the technique, "when your fingernails are clean and you can wash your hair and face, it'll make the day wash off. You feel like you can wash away anythin' ...the day's troubles and toils. What remains is cleanliness ...of the body and soul. And, you flat out feel better."

"Day is washed?" her little one asked.

Laughing softly, she patted the little head. "Yes, Polly. You can actually wash off a hard day and make yourself feel just a bit better."

"Oh, Mama!" the tiny voice responded. "I wanna wash off today!"

She frowned. "Why do you want to wash off today? Was it too hard?"

"No. Was so good! I just wanna wash a day."

Luraney laughed, her belly now bulging, and John smiled at his family.

And then Luraney, with the best cake of soap she had, taught her daughter how to wash off a day.

Butter ...how to make butter? She tried to remember the steps. *Churn, churn, and more churn. The fat in cream ...try not to agitate it too much ...it can badly separate and become ruined! Salt. Thank goodness for those two cows. Jeez, if these two cows didn't save my spirit!* She shook her head. It was unbelievable. *Who knew two dang cows—from Jobe no less!—could bring me to blossom?* Polly was at work milking the udders, while her mother agitated the fat just enough with the surprisingly smooth churn John had constructed for her. Lucky, she was a quick study here too.

Within days, with ever-increasing renewed vigor to bloom where her seeds were sown, with the milk from her precious cows, with the cleanliness of the lye soap made from the ashes of her own fireplace, Luraney had perfected the best butter she'd ever tasted. *Taste this! Is it better or worse than the batch prior? Creamier? Better? Ah yes ...that extra salt makes all the difference...* John tasted every batch, each one better than the previous. Proud of herself, she made extra thick biscuits every night that week for dinner and watched as her family devoured the melted drops of yellow heaven on their bread. *I think we just may make it here. And even thrive.* She thanked the Lord. The fire that night was warm and the battlefield within was at peace. A pioneer woman had been born.

ᴄ⌢Chapter Three⌢ᴐ

1819—MORE NEIGHBORS

Luraney's soap and butter production did not have to wait long for more customers. Joshua Jobe and his family flourished on their land, and so did the group he had brought with him. Now, even more new neighbors arrived in the isolated, beautiful mountain valley. The eagles made many appearances, almost every day, to greet the new humans as they arrived on their wagons, with horses, and with children in tow. Not just one eagle anymore, male and female had found one another. Swooping down over man's paraphernalia, the creatures were able to assess the fellow life forms.

Busy, wherever they were, trees fell, and green grass disappeared, homes rose, and some other animals stayed within fences. Some were large, milk spilling out of their undersides as the humans squeezed; some were low to the ground with curly tails, eating from troughs. Others, more familiar to the eagles but seeming never to fly, pecked on the ground, leaving trails of feathers everywhere. Day after day, peering down from their huge nest, laying upon their eggs, the eagles watched as the cove bustled with activity. The majestic birds recently detected that small game was harder to come by with all those souls out and about, but the creeks and lakes were still full of fish, their favored meal. Both eagle and man instinctively know, from early life, that they must recognize when to adapt. Life is ever-changing.

The Tiptons had arrived. The family was very welcomed as the Olivers knew them from their pre-cove days in that other part of Tennessee. Friendly, salt of the earth people they were; they'd fit in very well.

"Welcome! It's been too long!" Both families exchanged greetings and the Tiptons marveled at Luraney's pregnancy and little Polly's good manners and helpfulness. "Wow, what a place y'all got here!" The newcomers took in the natural beauty, and man's taming of it in the form of crops and homestead. "Amazin' ...and it ain't even been that long y'all have been here!"

Luraney thought, *"You don't know the half of it. It hadn't been but half a year, but that first winter, I coulda swore lasted a decade or more .... "*

The two families caught up with one another, accompanying the Tiptons as they toured the entirety of the cove in their wagon, seeking a solid homesite in the Southside of the enclosed bowl. John pointed out the southerly area's attributes and need to get away from the swampy sites. Good, solid land, tucked amongst lush trees. *Yes, this was the place,* the entire Tipton family agreed, and stepped from their wagon and horses to get down to work.

"A home, a barn, fencing, gardens, crops…" John was in constant talk that day, telling his old friend and new neighbor the work that lay ahead. "There's a heckuva lot to do. But you know, I will help wit' anything I can. We're all one big family here. Lots of great neighbors. All reliable and friendly. We ain't got no one but ourselves." He paused, seeing their faces fall just a tad. Then, he continued, solemnly; the realities justifying his warnings. "If one isn't a hard, self-sufficient worker, you'll die within a fortnight. But if one has an ...*ingrained* and strong work ethic, well, one's life here in this cove will be rich and adventurous ...even magical."

The Tiptons, warmly greeted by the original family of the cove, had the distinction of being the first white settlers to enter the land legally.

"Y'all know you have a real claim to your land?" John told his old friend. "And that south side area is prime land ...y'all can really spread out there."

"Indeed, I heard that. They told us when they issued me the land grant. 640 acres. And more comin'."

John whistled. "That's some solid land, Tipton."

He nodded in thanks. "Can't wait to get the crops goin'. But it don't matter ...the legality of it. I know that you, John, have as legal a claim as I do to your land."

"Agreed. Thank you for that. My land is mine. Forever. Jobe assured me of that. Or I'da never come here. But that Calhoun Treaty—just signed earlier this year ...I still can't believe it's 1819 already .... Anyways, we heard it was agreed to and signed by the Cherokee Indians to transfer their land to the State. Our Tennessee just got bigger."

"Yep, I heard 'bout that too. Big news actually. That John Calhoun, the Secretary of War, negotiated the deal—somethin' like the state'll pay the Cherokees for their land. And, them Cherokees, they figured since there was white men on their land anyway, they may as well be paid for it."

"Hmmm .... Interesting how they're businessmen too. You know, they saved our lives that first winter."

"Is that so?" Tipton asked, surprise written on his face.

"It is. Completely. Brought us food. They're good people. Very good."

"Hmm. Well, since it's you this is all comin' from John, I believe you."

With much negotiation between Tennessee's Secretary of War and the Cherokee Indians, the men agreed to and signed the historic Calhoun Treaty, but like most agreements in history; there were trepidations, excitement, regrets, and certain built-in flexibility and practicalities. Crops, being the lifeline of all people, were allowed to still be cultivated in the area and was specifically stated in the treaty: "The United States, in order to afford the Cherokees who reside on the lands ceded by this treaty, [shall grant] time to cultivate their crop next summer..."

For now, the Indians basked in their land money; money they'd never had before. Their crops were not in the cove proper and the two peoples did not overlap in their production of food and livelihood. Of course, it was heartbreaking to sell their ancestral lands, and much sorrow was felt. The twelve Cherokee who visited John and Luraney's lonely little cabin during last winter's sufferings did return one time to say goodbye.

"Nvwatohiyada." They said, bringing dried herbs and nuts as a gift.

"We wish you peace as well." John had replied, accepting the gifts and handing the large Cherokee four cakes of Luraney's best soaps.

"Ola" *Soap.* Surprised, they fingered the slick squares and smiled. Nodding to one another, they passed the cakes around, rubbing their arms and scalps in pretend washing. Held them to their noses and sniffed ...eyebrows raised in pleased wonder.

"Uwoduhi." *Beautiful.*

Luraney felt a special pride at her gifts of luxury to the Indians.

They shook hands and waved goodbye to one another.

"I wonder where they'll go." Luraney asked softly. "Well, they can still stay and tend their crops ...as the treaty says ...they must be 'round here somewhere, perhaps o'er those northern peaks."

"We've seen 'em comin' from the West a lot...perhaps they're over there."

"Maybe they're all around us..."

The Cherokees felt heartbreak, but they were also a very practical people ...and very forward-thinking. Like the eagle, they instinctively knew, from early life, that they must recognize when to adapt. Life is ever-changing.

The Calhoun Treaty was lucrative for both sides, but especially for the newly arrived Tipton family. It meant land opening up for sale, increasing State revenue and providing more and more opportunities for families like the Tiptons to buy and consolidate land for their very own.

"Hey, John! Great news for us Tiptons!"

"What's doin'?" he asked, as he walked up and stood on one side of William Tipton's newly erected fence. It was a beautiful spring day, one where the breezes swept the valley clean of frets and worries. Wildflowers were beginning to show their color and bees buzzed the entire area, pollinating swaths of fields.

"Remember us talkin' about my land grant? Was done on March 21, 1819—seems like just yesterday don't it?—when we were granted the very first Tennessee land grant for the cove?"

"Oh, I recall alright. Again, congratulations William!" John was genuinely happy for his neighbor, patting him on the back of his baggy overalls. "Y'all surely arrived here in style!" he teased his friend.

"Well, I got an update for ya. Before I got here, I confirmed it of course, but I managed to consolidate some other land I had, and we just got it totally official ...1280 acres. *Two* sections of 640 acres each. Sold to me a $1.00 per acre."

"Golly, that means you own 'most of the bottom half of the dang valley!'"

"Indeed."

John thought about that. Remembering how he and Luraney simply showed up, staked out a place, built his homestead and farm, and all for free. He had paid nothing. No bothering with grants or legalities. Jobe had insisted that the state didn't care if people settled here, and so they needed no formalities. What was money anyway? Some made-up piece of paper that men fought wars over. Men fretted day and night over those pieces of paper and those puny circles made of stamped metal. What was it that Ben Franklin had said? Back in the Revolution days? "He that loves money most shall lose; his anxiety for success of the game confounds him."

Tipton has a growing family. At least three children now ...and surely more to come. John thought about his own growing family -*soon to be one more*- and understood the need for security and owning your own home. Land. Owning—that was key—no one can take it away. He understood this with complete certainty. Had fled here to this cove for just that very reason—he had no money and no home of his own and could never hope to make any being a collier. No, he *had* to come here to own his own land. There was no other way to it. No matter if he paid paper money for it or not—he worked it and tended to it and *believe you me, I paid for it plenty. My coffers are dry from paying with buckets of sweat, dirt, tears, brute strength, and the strongest desire to succeed that ever burned a man's soul.*

"Well, I'm happy for you, Tipton. Money is good to have, and you deserve it. But men here in the cove, the few of us that are here, we're never gonna be judged based on our money, but on our characters, our crop yields and our families."

"Well said, John. You Olivers ...you are very esteemed as neighbors and friends. I am honored to share this place with you. Dang ...it *is* beautiful...." he trailed off as he looked out over the fields, the peaks capped with brownish balds and trees pushing always to the sky. Two men became lost in the sheer magnificence of the mouth of the mountains.

"Jobe!" John yelled as he snapped to attention and saw his neighbor come into view. "Come on over!" Waving his hand in invitation.

Jobe strode across the fields and joined the two men.

"You look as full as a tick, Tipton!" Jobe laughed and slapped his father-in-law on the back. He was married to Ruth Tipton, William's daughter. "What's the news?"

They discussed the Calhoun Treaty for a bit longer. Indians. Land grants. Acreage. William's newly acquired land, and the way the cove community was growing. Money. Crop yields. Seeds. Cows. Women and guns. Men's talk.

When that was all worked out and there was a pause to look out at what they'd built thus far, Jobe offered, "Time for some folklore, John and Bill." Sit and listen, he said with a twinkle in his eye. He loved telling stories.

The men walked until they found some logs in a soft, shady spot amongst the pine needles, sat and listened to their friend, the one who pushed them both to come to this cove in the first place.

"When us whites moved in—those Spaniards of old startin' with De Soto, the "place of the river otter"—that's what the Cherokees call it—was renamed Kate's Cove to honor the wife of the Indian Chief at the time, named Abraham."

"You didn't know the story before! ' Least that's what you said." John accused. "When you all but told us to come here! Don't you have Luraney hear you ...she'll grab my Ol' Blue 'n go after you right, if she finds out you knew this story all along and held back."

Jobe laughed. "Oh, no way I ever tell your Luraney!" He tipped his head back and feigned choking. "Firecrackers and I don't mix!"

"Anyways, I know more of the story now because, when I was gonna come back...don't say it John, I know it took me longer than I'd planned ...when I was gonna come back, I made it a point to find out even more about where I was sendin' you ...and myself."

John was silent.

"So, the Chief 'round these parts—Chief Abraham—was also honored by the naming of Abrams Creek—he was grateful to us white men who came through here for huntin' and such, for honoring him that way. Back then you know, we didn't run all over one another. We didn't live here. We just lived our lives—theirs in their tepees and smoke-filled villages, and us, with our different clothes and homes made of wood far away. The cove just served as a pass-through for both of us. It worked."

He paused, looked at the men and continued. "Later, this ...majestic sliver of land we live in right now—this Cades Cove—was named that way to honor that Chief Abraham, and his wife was named Kate. Kate's Cove. Kate. Kade. Cades Cove."

"So Abrams Creek and our name, Cades Cove, both come from Chief Abraham. A Cherokee."

"Yep. That's right."

"Must've been a heckuva Chief."

John and Bill Tipton laughed and nodded in agreement at Jobe.

"But in all seriousness, right from the beginnin', honoring the land and its ancestors were important and something that John, you did, and Jobe, you too. And now," Bill Tipton suddenly turned solemn, "my family and I are gonna make sure we cherish our history that has already begun. It's part of our heritage and teaches us folks, and our kids, some respect—us white men and the red man—makes us think beyond just our own lives to the bigger picture. God put us together somehow...."

The men reflected for a moment. Indeed, they were all part of a legacy in the making. Something they knew would last a long time, beyond their own lifespans and even beyond the time people would live in the cove. It may not last forever, but they knew with full hearts that cultural contributions from both races of men, would. The profoundness of this was that all three of them knew it, without it even occurring yet.

William Tipton came from good stock. His father was Colonel John Tipton, a Revolutionary War Veteran, who brought his family from Virginia to the upper East Tennessee area, near Jonesboro, in 1782. William, who was fast coming to be known as *Fightin' Billy,* though he was a peaceful man, settled at the south end of the cove, where the Tipton family had an eye on for a long time, even before coming here permanently.

For it was the Tipton family that Joshua Jobe can credit for first hearing of the cove; after all, the Tiptons were his wife's family. He had married Ruth, William Tipton's daughter in 1808, demonstrating just how important closely-knit family ties were from these earliest dawning days of the mountain community. Marriages were spun from nearby families that all knew each other very well; much of the time, it was a matter of availability, but also of strategic diplomacy. *Can we combine our farms? We want to leave our homestead in good hands...both families are responsible members of our town... We need that family as our ally ...She is fair and can cook and sew ...He's a hard worker and can provide....*

Being that the Jobes and Tiptons were interlocked all the way back in 1808, why didn't William Tipton come immediately? Why was Jobe the one who pushed instead, the Oliver family to come here? Tipton had a lot of other business interests in Jonesboro and was not quite in the position to come to the cove in 1818. But now, in 1819, enough time had passed for things to fall into place, to consolidate some land, achieve the land grant; he had convinced his wife, and his children had grown just enough to make the move more enticing. They were old enough where, born and bred with dirt in their shoes, they could help on his farm. *The more hands, the better* ruled pioneer life.

For his part, Jobe had a burning desire to live in the cove and settle there, but he also wasn't quite ready in the fall of 1818; had to wrap up his job as Deputy Sheriff in a nearby town, and needed to finish some personal business. But why waste that time when he could help start settling the area without actually being there? He wanted to push people that he knew could thrive in the area to join him. And of course, in deciding who to push, if his wife's family wasn't quite ready, Jobe knew that his other good friend, John Oliver, was the one who was itching and scratching to make a home for himself, to own his own land, to pounce on any opportunity to make something of himself.

John was the one who seized the chance and took that crossing first.

"Oliver's Crossing," Tipton said to his friend, tipping his hat in John's direction. "now that's something."

No matter the timing, or how they came to cross over from their prior lives to the cove, here they were, all together now, standing in the middle of a gorgeous bowl of fertile land. It had all worked out. Despite new neighbors and kin affiliations arriving now and in the coming years, the cove remained mostly the Oliver's—perhaps not in total land area and property, but in that much more important role of leadership. *Oliver's Crossing* was the unofficial name they used amongst themselves. No one else outside of the fertile bowl knew that or used that name to refer to the area. It was theirs alone. Honored and Respected. Cherished.

The corn was growing tall and sturdy; John continued clearing the land, "one tree at a time, with his horse." He toiled from the very first wisps of sunrise until the last drops of day fell behind the mountains. "Crops of corn, rye, oats and vegetables grew in abundance," and John planted plenty. Pumpkins, never seen in the wild by the Olivers during winter, only brought by the savage Indians to save their lives, were now so abundant that John repeatedly marveled to anyone and everyone, "I can walk over the fields on them without ever touching the ground." Luraney and the neighbors smiled at the awe in John's voice when speaking of the pumpkins. He developed such a taste for the large, seedy, fruit with edible flesh! *Orange stepping stones*, they'd call them. Some were even green. Luraney had learned to make the most wonderful pumpkin pies, pumpkin puree, and, catching a bit of the pumpkin-fever from her husband, thought, *I can add them to my butter! Maple syrup, sugar ...a bit of apple juice...* And so, she experimented and added them to her wonderful butter to make pumpkin butter—quickly becoming the toast of the cove amongst the neighbors, who were always clamoring for batch after batch.

"Luraney, when Ruth comes home from your house with that pumpkin butter ...mmm hmmm ...there ain't nothin' more fetching!" Jobe declared. "I eat it right outta the jar!"

John was proud of his wife, entirely happy that she was so enterprising. "Your soap, butter, and now the best pumpkin butter in Tennessee—maybe in the whole of America—why, you have an outright general store startin' right here at the Oliver's!" He kissed her. She was always surprised at that rare show of affection and kissed him back. Feeling satisfied, she dipped the spoon into the jar and put a dab of the butter on his tongue. "Luraney, you have a gift. That is just so, so good."

"Thank you, John." And it sure felt good to have a bit of something to call her own.

Indeed, those pumpkins were life-savers in more ways than one, and John would never, ever forget their symbolism of hope, of sustenance and of existence. After all, there was a time that first winter, before the Indians brought the gift of the dried pumpkin when John ate the bark right off the dormant, leafless trees. While he was out hunting. He never told Luraney.

Their cattle, thanks to thoughtful husbandry, now numbered two more than the original two milk cows gifted to Luraney from Jobe. Two hundred, eighty-three days was the average gestation period for cows; it had only been a few months ...*Jobe knew that both of them were pregnant when he gave them to me*, Luraney realized. She was sure John realized it too, for he knew the ways of animals like he knew the importance of pumpkins. Oh, but she knew her husband too well. He didn't say anything for a reason, wanting instead for her to come to these conclusions on her own. *Maybe Jobe wasn't so bad. He tried his hardest to make up for leaving us here... Except for not returning when he should've, he's always been the model neighbor and friend* ....She laughed knowing that her husband knew full well she had a mind of her own.

The small herd was kept along "Abrams Creek, where they grazed on rich grasses during the summer and found forage and protection during the winter." Those cows provided much-needed nourishing milk, and from there, butter and cheese. And they grazed on the abundant land at nearly no cost. *Pumpkins and cows.* Luraney laughed at the thought of these two life forms—one appearing on leafy vines, the other walking around the creekside—coming together to make life better. To expand her world. *Life was easier with pumpkins and cows.* She smiled to herself while working in her garden, heavily pregnant now, under an easy summer sun. It had been a long time since she felt this good. Proud she was, of how far she'd come. *Life was good.* She stood up then, placed her fists into her back -*oh, this was going to be a big, healthy baby*- and walked over to a log to sit down for a bit. Polly was picking weeds, a great little helper she was! Luraney was content as her eyes soaked in the gentle breezes and earthy smell of her kitchen garden, of animals and of their growing crops. Her eyes fell on her home. With the smoke rising out of the chimney bringing enticing smells of the slow cooking stew for dinner, the sturdy fencing, the broom right outside the front door, the quilt drying in the sun .... *Home.*

The Oliver homestead now consisted of the still crude, but homey cabin, which was in a perfect location. John instinctively knew this when choosing the homesite, but it did prove to be absolutely ideal, because it faced the West which shielded the winter winds and summer heat. Further add-ons included the cantilever barn—a large "log barn with two animal pens and a threshing floor." This special threshing area was a smooth inside space for threshing grain with a flair, in order to separate the grain from the plant itself. This threshing floor also "provided space to store much of what would be their first ample harvest."

John had also dug a stone walled well sixty-four feet deep and wrapped the inside with smooth stones gathered from the fields. With the power of foresight and his well-known craftsmanship, he already knew, even at the time of construction, that this well, as he repeatedly told his neighbors and wife, "would never run dry even after a hundred years."

The kitchen garden, laid out right where Luraney was now taking a rest, was cultivated on a warm south slope convenient to the house. Filled with field greens, peas, cabbages, potatoes and onions, they'd provide the freshest of salads and sustenance for the family. The smokehouse huddled close to the cabin for protection from animals and the rare risk of hungry human intruders. Freshly killed deer, bear or turkey was always welcome, but more difficult to preserve for long periods of time. Pork was much easier to salt, smoke, preserve and store until the next hog-killing time ...ham, bacon, jowl, sausage and other products were hung in quantity and quality within their secure smokehouse. The Olivers may not have had their own pigs, but the neighbors sure had brought many overland on their wagons when they'd arrived. The close-knit community shared what they had, all too happy to swap out ham and bacon for Luraney's soap and butter.

The springhouse looked down on everything else on the homestead, ensuring a clean water supply, while the cantilever barn stood below all other buildings, so the animal smells would travel away from the cabin, the family could store equipment in the winter, and precious livestock could be sheltered during the windy, icy cold months.

A cabin, a water well, cattle, crops, garden, outbuildings, mostly all enclosed by fencing—the homestead was now well-built and well-established and the Olivers felt much better about their lives. There was an old saying amongst these early settlers: "They that lived amongst these logs was almost as much a child of the forest as the other beasts. They pressed close to the breast of the earth and danced with the seasons."

Indeed, the Olivers were beasts of the mountain, pressed close to the soil, and their lives fell in step with the rhythms of nature, the leaves falling, the ice accumulating, the flowers and blooms, and now, the sunlit rays of the heating season. It was in the thick of this pattern, this relaxed and secure atmosphere, well removed from the first winter, and with friendly and amiable neighbors around that Luraney felt the pangs that summer day, resting on her log in the easy sun in the middle of her homestead.

"Oh ...goodness .it's my time," Luraney moaned, clutching her belly. "Polly, can you go grab Pa? Right quick?" She tried to sound calm, but Little Polly immediately toddled to the fields where her father was. Just about two years old, she was one of the many children who grew up quickly in this world. Luckily, he was close by and saw little Polly running eagerly towards him. Polly was relieved to see her father so near, because she knew her mother was having a baby and even she sensed excitement. Without knowing much of anything yet, little children still manage to contain a profound awareness. She, of course, did not know that her father had remained on the north side of the fields, close by on purpose since he knew his wife's time was any day now.

John reassured his wife and ran as fast as he could for Ruth Jobe, and the Tipton women, but they had already seen John running towards their homesteads, and met him halfway across the cove, already carrying tin buckets, jars, and quilts. Mountain women were always prepared, for a live birth, or otherwise. They knew when a woman's time was close, and had been ready for weeks. They had herbs and ointments, and whiskey. They had food at the ready, hands to distract the younger children and to help with chores, and more whiskey. The rest, the women always said, was in God's hands, but whiskey made His decisions much easier to bear.

The women comforted Luraney, boiled water, looked after Polly, and urged just a bit more drink to ease the pain. Luraney did not like the drink, and insisted that John not imbibe too often or too much, which he didn't, but here, she succumbed to the warm alcohol swimming down her throat. The ease that soon washed through her insides. She secretly admitted—only to herself mind you - that it did work ...like magic.

"Stay away from the whiskey for most of your life. But when bringing *forth* life ...well, that's what it was made for." Ruth Jobe wisely counseled the others. And so, with the help of whiskey and God, after a difficult but relatively quick and safe labor, the sound of a baby crying was joyfully welcomed.

The Olivers happily welcomed their second daughter, Martha, in the mid-summer day of July 18, 1819. She was the first Oliver born in Cades Cove.

While the cove women and John were in and out of the homestead that wonderful day, giving updates, fetching things, keeping busy, and finally, announcing the joyful news to the gathered neighbors and friends, the eagle swooped down over the homestead many times, sensing a new life. The people noticed and were always awed by this living symbol of freedom, boldness, and strength. His mate remained at the nest, snuggling the two eggs, one of which would also hatch today. Nature was having a midsummer festival, creating an easy sun, smiling at both bird and being, all the while whispering *though she be but little, she is fierce.* Both bird and being brought life into the world today. Both girls. Both little. Both fierce.

"She is beautiful. God Bless Her." John held his newborn with tears in his eyes. Everyone had left and it was twilight. The eagle was back in its nest, his rightful place. The other egg would hatch tomorrow. Luraney had made it through—no guarantee even in the best of times—and he now had two healthy children. His family was growing, something farm families always relished and strived for. The more hands to help, the better for the entire family enterprise. Luraney looked at her husband and smiled. "We did it again."

"We sure did honey." A rare display of affection for a tough, self-sufficient mountain man. He smiled at his wife. "We did it. Two healthy children. A farm that sustains us.

Friends and neighbors. Food…" he sighed happily and stared into the soft evening fire.

"Cows and pumpkins…" Luraney teased her husband.

"Soap and butter!" He countered, but with a huge grin on his face. He took her hand, the one not cradling the newborn baby girl.

"Indeed, Luraney. With you, life is good.

The year 1819 ended in a much better place for the growing little cove family. There was no starvation, nor any fear of it. In fact, food was so abundant, they could afford to trade a bit. They traded with neighbors, but also with the wagon trains that came and went into the neighboring towns to swap for shoes, cloth, flour, sugar, and salt.

"John McCaulley over there on the south side tol' me he harvested a whole load of chestnuts. And then he went in his wagon….said chestnuts are gettin' $2.00 a bushel in Knoxville! He said he had enough to buy all his six children shoes for the winter!"

"Well, our corn …we're all lookin' to produce I'd say about 500 bushels this summer …we can surely sell that and buy ourselves all the things our wives say we need, and then some….maybe couple pieces of leather for horse upkeep, tools—maybe another scythe or two—and some tobacco."

The growing number of humans pressing close to the breast of the earth danced more eloquently and smoothly within its leaves, ice, creeks, and blooms. The Indians were nowhere to be found save for brief glimpses on the west and sometimes south side of the cove. Best of all, the Olivers were no longer alone, and in fact, from here on, the cove would prosper. It was a wonderful time.

Yet not every being would succeed.

The eagles perceived it, had a keen foresight; these new, pale men were here now all the time. And they kept coming and staying. Where did the original men go? The reddish-brown ones? The ones who slept under leathery triangles that flapped in the wind? They had never cleared land and made things grow in nice, even rows like these new men. Well, maybe they had a little bit, but not on the scale of the pale men. These new men were ...*new*. They did things differently. Yes, it was a prosperous time, a wonderful time. And, as the eagles watched in daily increments, it was all to the grave detriment of the ones who were here first.

Chapter Four

1821

"They're turnin' on us." John Oliver told Joshua Jobe. "Them Indians, they done turned on us white folk!" His folksy accent was very present now, coming out in raging force at times like these. He tried to rein it in some of the time, when he remembered, to sound more formal and businesslike, now that he owned his own farm. But when agitated, it flew like the tail of a dog.

"Indeed they have! It's just ...they're more of *us* now." Jobe relayed his thoughts one night while visiting John, Luraney, Polly and now little Martha—all looking quite well and happy. He couldn't believe how time flew! Little Martha was walking and talking ...Polly was her mother's fast-maturing helper. There had been other babies born in the cove too. The years swooped by while they were all leading very busy lives.

"When you was one little family, you weren't no threat. There was just you Olivers. They even felt sorry for you! But then, a few more ...me and my family and friends. But now ...even y'all number a bit more than two and a half and a quarter." He chuckled and smiled at Polly and Martha, Polly protesting she was not to be counted as only a half, but despite the tease, Jobe was dead serious.

John jumped in with his thoughts. "We *are* a bigger group. And I suppose, a bigger threat. We also are smarter. Just do things different from them. My opinion ...we been doing things right. We recognized the 'fertility of the soil, and the superior advantages in raising stock' that maybe they didn't. I don't know how they think, but we done it and they never did. And they been here so much longer!"

"Let's face it. We really transformed this place. Look around it's all fields! Not a lot of forest left. Not like it was anyways. I guess they don't recognize it anymore as it once was. Envy? Jealousy? I don't know ...I imagine they feel threatened. I mean, they were here for who knows how long? A long time. But did they ever cultivate the land like we did? No."

The cove had certainly passed from humble beginnings to an outright community—the makings of a town even—a hub for anyone traveling through these increasingly populated, yet still isolated parts.

"We don't really interact, though." John added, running his fingers through his hair and scratching his beard. "They live their lives. We live ours."

"True."

"I wonder when that changed. When they decided to turn on us. Because they have. Hearin' more stories of encounters lately. More aggression ...many don't run away now, or nod their heads and walk on, goin' on about their business. They run *towards* us and glare at us. Attacks on white folk while out huntin'. I heard of another one just last week ...."

"True, John. Somethin's changed. But maybe we can still live and let live. That seems to work."

"It does for a time. Until someone decides their way of life is dyin' and they're gonna take the rest of us out too."

The live and let live mentality worked, but was short-lived. The Cherokee Indians could be seen only very occasionally now, and they let the pioneers be for the most part. But as is true with any two peoples coming together; conflict arises. At first, somehow, both groups converge into a *simpatico* relationship -*let me be and we will let you be.* Mutual respect it's sometimes called and more people should have heeded that warning from the earliest of times. But humans aren't built for that. And it rarely happens. Aggressions become more frequent and violent. One group invariably overtakes the other. Greed, need, and speed all determine who overtakes first.

Jobe was one of the countless humans who have told this very same story, with only slight differences in the details, to their fellow man, during a cool and breezy Saturday summer dusk. Saturday evenings were visiting times; children explored homesteads together and adults shared food and caught up on news and happenings. The sky had tilted its head, revealing its rosy pink and orange cheeks, as Jobe continued his visit, pulling closer a cane rocking chair by John and Luraney's bright and warm fire. The Jobe and Oliver children were all gathered upstairs in the loft. They could hear their giggles and scurrying across the floor above. Ruth had walked south to fetch her father that evening but was expected soon, and so Jobe rounded up their numerous kids—they'd had nine by now—and walked over to the Olivers. He'd been there since late afternoon and he remained here this evening; in the mood to continue to talk Indians.

"They helped you that first winter? Do you want to know why?"

They heard activity outside, and Luraney peeked out, unlatched the door. Ruth and her father William Tipton were walking up the gravelly pathway. Tipton had spoken to John earlier in the week about the cove's fast-changing dynamics. Really, the only topic of conversation lately *was* the escalating situation with the Indians. And so, John had invited his neighbors over to discuss it further. The men needed to get a grip on the situation. There was nobody else around to help and assistance was days, if not weeks, away. Perhaps help would never be sent. Their good sense, fairness, and rifles were all they had.

"God helps those who help themselves."

"Proverbs?"

"No, Ben Franklin."

The men chuckled at John's ever-present religious views, but his even stronger practicality.

"Ben Franklin's Virtues: Temperance, frugality, humility…"

"I recall silence in there somewhere!" Tipton, his good-humored fighting spirit erupted into laughter.

"Industry!" John exclaimed with a smile, chuckling, but then steering them back. "Okay. Let's not waste time!" He slapped his knees and rose from his chair. "Need to get to the problem at hand…we need a solution."

As the sky brushed off its rosiness and tucked itself in for the night, the children had gone to bed, or at least, they were all up the rickety stairs to the top floor, huddled under the quilts in their beds of hay. They listened closely though, because that was how they learned what it was like to be an adult, and because what did their parents always say? *Small*

children, small problems. Big children, big problems.
And so they listened silently and learned.

"Because it was only you. No one else," Jobe answered
his own question on why the Indians helped them during that
first, starving winter.

Jobe continued. "Y'all heard this before. It was only
one family. You. We know that. But then—we've been over
this too—more of us white men and our families came." He
paused. "But what we never said ...let's be serious now—is,
we *took* their land, their food, all the trees from them. Look at
this place! We've cleared it through and through. The Indians
are becoming hostile and now, we'll never be friendly again.
Y'all know this I think, but it begs repeatin'—they even killed
my uncle!"

With that, a not-surprised but suddenly gasping
Luraney, who was puttering around the front porch and house
with Ruth, straightening up, talking gardens, and pretending
not to get involved with men's talk, went inside and walked to
the fire. She and Ruth Jobe sat on the bed, while the men sat in
the cane-backed chairs.

John got up slowly and stoked the dry, spitting logs,
knowing what they would hear out of their neighbor's mouth
as he told the story again. *Jobe the storyteller.* They all had
mixed feelings, especially John and Luraney. Still fearing the
Indians just a bit if they were honest ...yet how could they
forget the brown man's—or red as Luraney called them-
immense kindness? They had saved their lives! What human
could ever forget? She had even looked for them, praying for
them to appear over the snowy ridges, their tall figures
signaling kindness.

The fire crackled with another fresh log, and they all listened, again, while Jobe recanted the tale. Unbeknownst to the adults, the children crept to the base of the ladder and lent their ears to these grassroots lessons of history.

"They lingered in small bands, in the mountain vastness ...all went well for a while." Jobe chewed on his lip before continuing. Ruth looked down at her folded hands. "Indians could be seen only occasionally prowling around, but would soon leave, and get back into the deep mountain gorges. Game being plentiful, my uncle was out hunting one day and had wandered farther than usual into the mountains, and did not return that night, and when search was made for him the next day he was found in a deserted Indian camp, on his knees leaning up against the side of the camp- slumped- where he had been murdered by the Indians. They had cut off one of his fingers and fled."

The group was silent, once Jobe was finished with his fast and formal, stream-of-consciousness recounting, reflecting again on how, when two peoples collide, it rarely works out for both groups.

None of the settlers knew then that the Indian threat would end in 1838 when the Trail of Tears forced the remaining Indians to Oklahoma. And none knew then— certainly not John Oliver—that he—the one whose very life was saved by the kindest of Cherokees—would be among the local militia charged with the final roundup of these remaining Indians.

The children looked at one another, crept back into bed, and remembered forever that the Indians chopped off fingers.

The Jobes, the Tiptons, and the Olivers all sat in their own thoughts. They had all crossed through here tonight, this small dwelling made of wooden ribs of the earth, warmed by the harnessed energy of fire licking the hearth's walls, the group silent, as Nature herself witnessed the inner thoughts and conflicts of this tiny group of cove residents. And in her infinite wisdom about what was to happen, and about her inability to stop man—itself a part of her vast and compromising repertoire—she did not interfere.

With almost the sole "exception of his uncle's murder"—having made such an indelible impression that it became legend, being retold around each hearth time and time again—Joshua Jobe led an idyllic picture of life in the cove during the 1820s. Corn, "although cheap at six and one-quarter cents per bushel," he lamented, "was the main crop," as he told friends and family in letters, urging them to come to the cove and build their Cades Cove community. And corn grew so abundantly, along with other staple crops, "that when the oak leaves were as large as a squirrel's ear," they knew it was time to plant, plant, plant, day and night, absolutely guaranteeing a robust crop. Young girls looked for blood-red corncobs amongst the usual yellow ones, ensuring they'd be next to marry. Young boys secretly planted some of these special corn seeds to ensure that girls would find them on his family's land and thus, look to them to marry. Corn dolls cropped up amongst the younger children, but the mothers and aunts thought they reeked of Indian rituals, and therefore tried to hide them as much as possible.

Fruit, save for some apples and berries that they assumed the Indians planted, were imported so the men of the cove could plant and nurture orchards of their own, but once introduced, were plentiful. Game, deer, bear, and smaller animals were in ample supply. Jobe even had a "pet bear" which was both treacherous and astonishing.

"How's your bear?" the other children would ask Jobe's children. "He's gettin' large, but he's tame and gentle. But let me tell you ...he'd get loose once in a while, but one night, we ain't seen him for days. That night, my brother and I were sleepin' and it came through the window! It scared us badly! But as soon as he drank a churn-full of buttermilk, he went out the window and was roaming around about the barn at daylight. Then, he got into a bee swarm. Now, I have heard people say a bear could not be hurt by bees stingin' them, but it's a mistake." They all listened closely because they *had* heard that myth.

"Well, our pet bear got in a knot of bees, but they bit him and he wiped them off with his nose, but the bees kept stingin' him and he began to holler and rip and tear. He broke his collar and away he went into the woods."

"Did he come back?"

"Oh yeah, he came back. Stung up real good. But he came back."

Jobe, his children, and the rest of the growing population of young residents were more than just mountain families in the wilderness trying to eke out a living in the utopian harshness of the cove. In addition to tending to pet bears, and working the fields and homesteads with their parents, education was prioritized and the children attended school which, even outsiders agreed, was surprisingly rigorous.

"One thinks that a rural, secluded cove community would not have rigor, or would not have much need for education." The women lamented to the men during their frequent neighborly meetings in the middle of the cove. The sun shone at an angle, thanks to the blockages of mountaintops, making their meeting spot shaded, yet warm.

"From what I've heard from back home," Tipton's wife exclaimed, "education in our parts, here in 1825, is more common sense and reasonable, better adapted to the needs and wants of the people than the curriculum of those studies that are generally taught now in the higher schools."

Education in the cove was indeed thorough and demanding. Practical. Which made better farmers, thinkers, leaders, and people. John Oliver, the big fan of Ben Franklin, again quoted his idol: "Tell me and I forget, teach me and I may remember, involve me and I learn."

Nodding heads met John's gaze and he continued. "Now that's the way to an education that could do any man or woman good."

"Indeed," everyone agreed. "The teaching that's going on here is engaging, and involves our ..." John struggled for the right words, then just told it simply. "Our *lives*. Our *real* lives."

Jobe continued the collective thoughts. "Think on it ...we have to calculate the prices of corn, figure out how much wood we need, the spacing of our crops ...but we also need to look to the moon cycles, observe our surroundings. No other schools have to watch Indians for their movements like we do. Our youngin's need this. They're not in the city, or town. We're—*they're*— here in the cove. All alone save for us few. Yes, observation is the best teacher."

"Indeed. And observation, combined with reading, writing and arithmetic, makes for a strong and smart mix." Most of their children were in school at that very moment, learning what they needed to learn no matter if they made their way to work in the bigger cities, or if they stayed here to work a cornfield.

"We are doin' right by our kids. They need to be educated as to where and how they live and to bloom where they're planted. And they're planted right here. But they can also be uprooted and planted anywhere else."

"And grow straight and tall right alongside the rest of 'em."

And with that final statement, Tipton's wife waved goodbye and walked away. The rest of the residents got back to planting and tending their fields.

The Olivers, Jobes, and Tiptons, amongst other cove settlers during the early 1820s, were close neighbors and friends and even became relatives of one another, just like they'd hoped. John and Luraney welcomed even more children, and by 1829 when Elijah was born, the Olivers were a happy and healthy clan of seven: John and Luraney, Polly and Martha, and Elizabeth, born in 1822, Lazarus—their first son—born in 1827, and Elijah, another son, born in the year, 1829.

Luraney and John were certainly busy, tending the farm and homestead, and feeding and clothing all of their beloved children. Luraney made more soap and butter than she'd ever seen. Like workers in a hive, they were buzzing around the gardens, crops, homes, corncribs, schools, and everywhere in between every single day, yet all was harmonious; each family's success depended on such generous and kind qualities. Isolation demanded working together and helping one another in times of want and in times of need. And they all genuinely liked one another, spending much needed time alone on their own lands, yet gathering around fences and hearths. They were all of like minds, no extremes or outliers, no one isolationist nor unfriendly. It was close to perfect.

"But everyone has a bad egg here and there," Luraney said one night to her husband. The crops and animals were doing well, the children were growing big and strong, and they had plenty to eat. Her soaps and butter were the toast of the community and her life was very content now. She enjoyed her life! She loved making homemade products and taking care of her dear children, husband, and neighbors in this utopian land where the eagles soar and the land provides.

And she hated anything disrupting that.

Luraney was worried about the escalating tension between Jacob, the son of William Tipton, and pretty much everyone else. Jacob was "the first bully of the cove," as they were all coming to refer to him as. It is interesting that his father, William, was known as "Fightin' Billy" Tipton, who, despite the moniker, wasn't known to be violent at all within the cove. In fact, he was a solid citizen, a peacemaker, and never made trouble.

"His spawn is another story." Luraney couldn't help spewing out the words.

"When Jacob bought land from his father in 1824 and then added to it, we all thought he was on his way to being a sorta community leader," John answered his wife, mirroring what Jobe told him earlier in the week. The young man who brought such tension to the harmonious little band of residents was the talk of the cove.

It was later in the evening and the fire crackled in the fireplace. Sighing deeply, John stood Ol' Blue in the corner and sat down with his wife, the smells of the earlier dinner lingering in the log cabin. He wiggled his toes in his socks and stretched his arms over his head. The children were upstairs asleep in the loft. Or were they? They lately seemed awfully mature for their tender ages.

John did not like bullying or dissent in the tiny cove community. After all, with few available resources, one bad seed could greatly disrupt the little group and prove lethal to both residents and the community as a whole. Luraney chimed in.

"Well, he is...Justice of the Peace and his house over there is the voting place when the 16th Civil Circuit was established." Jacob Tipton had certainly become an important member of their community, and she reiterated all his accomplishments. Then, she lowered her voice and gave her rebuke. "For the life of me, I don't know how *that* happened!"

John smiled at his wife's passionate spirits coming out. "True. He is very hot-headed. He fights first, then asks questions."

"Benjamin and Thomas—you know, William's brothers—they talk of their nephew Jacob as a loose cannon."

"Yes indeed." John agreed. "Because his daddy owns much of the cove and now he does too, it's done gone to his head."

"He *is* very domineering. Kind of always had that character if you think back on it," said Luraney, now not holding her tongue very well. "And he got worse. Now, he thinks his wealth makes him better. Well, not around here it don't. He's nothin' but a bully. And a stupid one at that. Tries to run with the big dogs, but really, his courage stays under the porch." They discussed how to handle the bully well into the night. Elaborate plans, all.

"William ...*Fightin' Billy* ...Tipton ..." she sighed, "He knows it full well too. So, that leads me to believe, even he's not sure what to do with his own son."

He nodded, looking into the dying fire. Thinking.

"What would *you* do?"

John was thoughtful for a moment, then in one of those rare moments of affection, rose from the chair and walked over and kissed his wife. "Lucky for me...you gave me a lot of daughters!"

"Oh, John!" Luraney laughed. And she knew what he was thinking: they did have sons, but he hoped he wasn't raising those sons to ever be burrs in the saddle. He hoped that between the two of them, they would sow their sons' seeds early on, and tend to them often, making sure they grew tall and strong and into God-fearing men.

"We all seen it, John. Happens rarely, but it happens. That even the best of the good farmers can plant bad seeds."

Nothing was set in stone that night, but the Olivers resolved to get Jobe involved, and were determined that they wouldn't let Jacob Tipton—the bad seed planted from a good farmer—dictate the neighborly atmosphere of the cove that they all worked very hard to maintain. Indeed, they would have to make elaborate plans to eradicate the crow in the cornfield. She wondered about the people that they'd have to gather, the planning, the meetings, these dark nights when they listened for any crack of twigs around the house.

Not a day or two later, before John even had a chance to address the issue with anyone, Jobe came running up the Oliver's pathway to the cabin in a panic. "Jacob! He done gonna...gonna kill....come.... Oh Lord!"

Luraney came running out of the cabin, Polly and Martha in tow, the older children outside weeding the garden, the little ones still inside playing with scraps of fabric. John had also heard Jobe's yells and was running back to his home from the fields.

"Jacob!" He repeated, out of breath. Bent over, he put his hands on his knees, catching his breath, and his words. "He came up to me ...out of nowhere and for no good reason, and grabbed me by the throat!" He gasped just relaying the story.

"Oh Lord!" exclaimed Luraney.

John arrived and sucked in his breath. He knew this was bad for the striving community. Very bad.

"He was going to choke me. Right then..." he stopped to catch his breath. "Right then, I happened to be whittling a stick with my pocket knife. Well, I tell you ...when he got me 'round the throat, I took my knife and cut Jacob's throat from ear to ear."

Luraney cried out and pushed her hands to her mouth. "Oh Lord. Lord..." she muttered.

"Did he...?" John was afraid to ask.

"No," Jobe said, settling down a little.

"He threw me down and jumped on me. God, he would've beat me unmercifully—he had six ruffian accomplices with him, mind."

"Oh Lord," Luraney could picture the scene. Poor Jobe with Jacob and six other bullies! How did he survive? And who were these other bullies and where did they come from? Probably from those over in Chestnut Flats! Luraney couldn't help but think that these people were way worse than any Indians.

Jobe continued the story, catching his full breath now. "Ruth ran out of the house with her club and dealt him two or three blows. He actually jumped up and kicked at her!" Luraney's horrified face stared back at him.

"But they fought back. By this time, I threw a rock at him, but he hit me in the stomach, causing me to vomit all over the place."

John sat down on the front porch, wondering how they would rid themselves of this stench in their community. Every place had at least one. Every country, county, city, town, cove, family, even household ...there was always one. Eventually. "God, I hope that doesn't happen to our family." John and Luraney looked at each other and both shuddered at the thought.

"I had *had* it with that ...that ...*snake* in the grass! You know, they *still* came after me. Can you believe it? They grabbed a large rock that they had to throw with both hands! I dodged it. Luckily." Luraney sat down on a log, shooing the children away for now with a bucket and instructions to fetch water from the creek. But the creek wasn't that far away, and they lingered, trying to listen to this big problem.

"And luck was still on my side when I noticed a large lump of clay that had fallen out of the kitchen chimney ...I aimed a dreadful lick at him..."

He calmed now, much more at ease relaying the terror. He even smiled wryly before the Olivers who, he saw, were spellbound and horrified, desperately wanting to hear the outcome. They knew he had survived ...after all, he was here telling the story. But still, it was ...otherworldly. Such worthless violence!

"I knocked out five of his teeth, split his upper lip to his nose, and mashed both upper and lower gums in a frightful manner. He lay covered with blood from his throat, but he still didn't want to give up!"

"My goodness! What happened then? How did this *ever* end?" Luraney had her hand to her mouth, incredulous, waiting to hear a very detailed plan. *Just when things were going well...*

To which Jobe replied in a matter-of-fact tone, no malice to be heard:

"I got my gun."

The eagle watched the pale men fighting one another. Actually, to be fair, it seemed that only one of the men was truly the instigator, like a blue jay in the nests of doves. Rocks were thrown, sharp talon-like metal blades flew, nothing stopped that one man. Except when the tall one pointed a long wooden stick at the aggressor, shouting deathly threats; that seemed to finally stop it all. Afterward, the eagle landed on the ground, curious, and sniffed the iron from the pool of red blood. It smelled like the fish they caught in the creeks when they would grip the slithery creatures in their talons before delivering it to the nest to eat. Tilting his head to peer up and around, all was quiet; yet not even a breeze could sweep away the shocked mood of the men. The bird shook out its feathers and flew away towards the creek.

In the coming weeks, Jacob Tipton recovered but was left severely injured. Unexpected and unwanted, this violent turn of events, he actually felt and showed remorse for the first time in his life. *I was just showin' off. Kickin' around with my friends. We drank a bit. I never wanted it to go this far.* He felt shame, something he may not have felt if he'd lived in a bigger town or area. But here, in Cades Cove, he had to get along with others. A requirement for such a small number of people who relied on no one except themselves. It was a tough lesson, one he confessed to his mother one night while his jaw was still throbbing.

"You *do* have to try to get along with everyone, Jake. We're a small group here. Do you want to live like this forever?" she admonished. "Your 'forever' was almost over starin' down Jobe's barrel ...you nearly died!" She had tears in her eyes.

Jacob, for once, sheepishly agreed with his mother. He was scared. "I know I'm a hot head sometimes...but..."

"My boy." She interrupted, rubbing his cheek gently with some wood nettle to promote blood flow, his entire face and neck still very black and blue. "You must make this right."

He nodded sheepishly as his mother rose, going to get some beefy soup for her errant son.

"I'll get with your daddy and arrange a meeting. We must make peace. For your sake and for the whole family's sake." Jacob grudgingly agreed, grumbled just a little, as expected, but he knew his mother, and his father, were right. He didn't have a lot of people on his side, and this was his home. He did love it here in the cove, and in order to stay, he'd have to straighten up. Eat a little crow, and put his shallow anger aside. Stop drinking. Do as his mother had been repeating to him for some time now: *Grow up, Jacob.*

Yes- he told himself ...*eventually* ...his jaw still throbbing, that surly spirit still wanting to hang around his heart. *Used to think the sun rose just to hear me crow.* But that gun barrel had a way of setting the rising sun faster than an eagle's scream. Jacob finally understood that his wild ways and bad behavior would do him in; next time it *would* be forever. At the very least, it would get him nowhere, no more power, no prestige, no friends, no more land...nothing ...It can no longer be: *I will grow up eventually,* he told himself. *Now. I must grow up now.*

The meeting went well. Though Luraney had snuck up behind a tree in the east to watch, never telling John she'd taken their other rifle named Ticker *just in case*, she was still able to act surprised when John told her what had happened. Men's work, they had said, telling the women to stay behind with the children just in case anything erupted again. One and all carried their best guns.

"Well, as you know, we all agreed to meet at a neighbor's home, which was halfway between their respective homes and agreed to settle differences. Jacob actually said—to everyone's surprise, "I promise to ever afterward live in friendship."

"D'ya think he meant it?"

"You know. I was suspect at first, of course. But I do. I do think he meant it. He seemed ...changed. And if he didn't mean it, them gun barrels just may do him some reminding for his own good." He smirked just a little bit, putting Luraney more at ease, for she'd seen it all, but hadn't heard any words. "Ol' Blue and the others were very convincing."

And he did mean it. Save for a few other relatively minor tiffs between others who he wanted to "lick," Jacob Tipton, son of the peaceful *Fightin' Billy*, never forgot his horrific injuries or his mother's advice. For the most part, he kept his word, though, not surprisingly, he was never fully trusted in the community.

War and peace—they dance together splendidly; no other spirits can compete against them. A love/hate match works for both sides; hardly a perfect match, nonetheless the mix perseveres and has a staying power that can outlast anything at all. All human civilizations have proved this point. The warring Jacob turned out to bring an oddly special peace and resolve to the cove; in fact, the neighbors helped each other even more, being kinder, visiting more often, and outwardly acknowledging their appreciation of one another. Together, they had solved every problem thus far. In turn, Jacob was surrounded by peace, assisting his offending spirit towards harmony. Thereafter, crisscrossing the cove each and every day, the Olivers, Jobes, and Tiptons—even with their bad seed sown from a good farmer—managed to live in calm in their prospering cove community.

Chapter Five

Late 1820-1830s

Cove life in the summer lull was all about picking berries. Blackberries grew in fields in such abundance that they seemed to attract all the bears in the area fattening up for the future. The best blackberry cobblers on earth could be found in this beautiful valley. Then, the blueberries came into season and were gathered and made into pies, jams, and preserves and eaten right off the bushes by the children. Small blue fingers were a must during the sun's hottest days.

In addition, the summer gardens of vegetables, field greens, peas, potatoes, cabbage, and onions gave Luraney and the other women plenty to do. Pulling weeds was a full-time job in and of itself. Keeping critters away was a constant challenge. It was a perfect task for children and the Olivers' and other families' children would run from farm to farm, across the cove, tending this garden or that one. The corn and wheat were growing, and the men, in between tending their farms and putting away hay, tended to the domestic animals, hunted squirrel, deer, rabbits, wild turkey, and even bears, and though bears were often hunted just for sport, the inhabitants of the cove did use them for grease and oil.

Cades Cove was a working garden of Eden ...for those who stayed. "There were some people who moved in and became restless; however, those who remained in Cades Cove became more cohesive, bound by a common manner of life. But it wasn't an easy life. The people worked hard and enjoyed their pleasures when they could. How they lived and passed their days" became a full-on mountain culture. There was very little cash used in the cove; there was no need for it, except for selling their corn, and other crops and goods in Knoxville and other towns. Even then, the cash was typically used right then and there, for shoes, tools, and other essentials not available in the cove. The wagons would leave heaped with corn and return full of new cloth, coffee, and shiny new boots for every child of a family. But that was an infrequent event—after harvests of course; otherwise perhaps only once or twice per year.

Each family was very self-sufficient right here in Cades Cove; they grew, raised, or hunted their own food. Sewed their own clothes, carding wool and spinning it into yarns to weave into cloth. The children, both girls and boys, were taught to quill the thread for the shuttle of the loom and spinning wheel. Many a night, Luraney would be industrious at her loom, churning out what seemed to be endless cloth to be turned into shirts, pants and dresses for her large family.

Additionally, they sold and traded amongst themselves, and made sure everyone was well fed. Luraney's soap and butter were especially sought-after, but generally, each family was responsible for their own. They passed their days in tough, but noble work that "was central to family life." But it wasn't all work. They made time for fun and freedom. When they weren't learning the ways of the land from their fathers, the young mountain men sometimes lazed around the creeks for an afternoon, languidly catching fish for dinner. "Leisure time was a premium to be cherished."

It was during this precious, premium, leisure time that they were able to greet their newest neighbor, Robert Shields. Word had spread about the exceptionally beautiful isolated, fertile cove and its success in growing premium corn. Robert had heard about it for some time now, and the more he thought of the idea, the more he realized he not only wanted to go but had to. For the sake of his family's safety and very survival, it was the right time to make his move.

There was a figure coming almost directly from the south, whose newest homestead was almost straight across the valley from the Olivers. The figure appeared to be in a hurry, with a clear purpose. As he got closer, they could see it was Robert Shields, and he seemed agitated—unlike him as he was usually calm as a dove. What was going on?

"I've come from Chilhowie. Now, don't be alarmed." Shields held his hand up and cautioned his newest neighbors as he hurriedly walked up to them. They had a chance meeting earlier last week, but between establishing the new homestead and all the initial chores that went with it, they hadn't truly had a chance to greet each other and talk in a meaningful way. And it didn't look like it was going to happen now either.

But of course, the established families already knew all about him. Knew his background very well. Robert Shields. A well-respected man. They had no doubt he would become a well-loved member of the cove. Having a business mind, with an eye towards improvements, he had purchased 1600 acres of land from William Tipton, and soon thereafter, moved his family to the cove to establish a homestead. Determined to make a mark in his new community, he already had many plans to improve and enhance conditions, and couldn't wait to get involved in everything cove related.

Of course, Shields came from good stock in the first place, something that mountain people greatly coveted and actively sought out. His father was a Revolutionary War Veteran, who "had built a fort at the base of a mountain because this territory was still contested by the Cherokee." The Cherokees were a sore spot for Shields because a son and some of his kinfolk—from the previous generation, "were killed by Indians while watering their horses outside a fort that was built at the base of Shields Mountain." Later, settlers would call the area Pigeon Forge.

They never knew if there was an altercation, or if one group was the aggressor. They never knew if the Indians felt threatened, or if they attacked. Or if his relatives felt threatened and attacked. The land was hotly contested by the Indians, and the situation was certainly tense enough for his father to build a fort as a lookout and shelter. But no matter the circumstances, his father would never again pass by the fort, or the base of the big tree right outside the fencing that saw it all, without grieving heavily. The tree soaked up their red, flowing blood, lifting the drops right up into the heart of the trunk, letting it surge into the greenest of summer leaves. Throughout his life, Robert's father would tell him that he would stand under the shade of that very tree and tears would mix with the dried blood at the base. It was the only way he could become one again with what happened—for one of them was his very own son—if only for a heartbreaking, killingly joyful moment. Sighing as he always did, Shields' father believed God would get him through, and he had to believe He had a plan. Why He had to plan it all with his own son and another relative being brutally killed was still beyond him ...and if you were honest with yourself, beyond every other human on earth. But that is what faith is.

Part of a hearty people and yearning for the good versus evil balance of life, Shield's father relayed to his son happy memories as well. And there were many. He'd always rave about the area of the cove. *Kate's Cove,* he'd say, *is profoundly fertile and ideal. It's the most beautiful place on earth. Son, if you can get there, you should.*

Proud father he was. In due time, as his father's son, Robert Shields moved his family from the fort area into the cove proper to begin his ambitions. There was one problem though. The happenstance for him moving here now was all wrong. Oh, he'd *wanted* to come here to the cove's welcoming bosom with all his heart. But he also *had* to.

"Hello," panting, he finally stopped at Oliver's homestead. Catching his breath, he hurriedly continued, not waiting for the usual exchange of pleasantries.

"Don't be alarmed," he repeated, "But there's a typhoid epidemic in Chilhowee."

"That's only 50-60 miles away!"

"Indeed, ma'am. We fled here. Had to get my family away from there. No worries, ma'am, we didn't bring any sickness with us. But there's too many of us ...I've got three children and a wife ...just couldn't risk 'em." he said matter-of-factly.

"Goodness!" Luraney said upon meeting Robert Shields, walking over to the tall man and shaking his hand. "We understand and am glad y'all are well. We welcome you to our little community." And she did welcome him with warmth and sincerity. But secretly, she was scared for their little cove community which now boasted 271 residents, including her husband and her daughters and sons. So were the other women, of which there were many, and, as women do, especially when frightened, they made their plans.

"There's poisonous vapors in the air. We must set the woods on fire."

It was approaching the late-1820s and the Cades Cove residents were sure they had figured out that decaying tree stumps or strange substances or *something* was making the air "rotten"; therefore, they had to be burned. No knowledge of bacteria or disease transmission was commonplace then. People just knew that fever, stomach pain, not wanting to eat, and headaches pronounced the coming of the typhoid illness. And they knew it passed from person to person.

Robert Shields, William Tipton, the Jobes, and Luraney and John Oliver stood around the middle of the cove that day talking about typhoid and what they knew: "old dead tree trunks held it in and then spread it around with the wind," or "when the breezes blew warm and the swamps grew fetid, we know to look out for the fevers." Robert told them the fever followed many, the dust lingering in their very breaths. And so, he came here, disease-free, of course. It's been a couple weeks since we arrived and we're sure to be disease-free."

Wary, the ladies didn't want to chance it. Why, something like this could wipe out entire families! And so, they got to work. Knew exactly what to do. Banding together, they set about setting small fires in the woods, spreading lime around their homes, drinking pine knots placed in their water, and hanging onions around the home. If you'd already been infected, perhaps half a chicken on the soles of the feet would suffice to "pull the fever out." All of this done with complete confidence, the women controlled the fears of the cove residents very well.

With so much to do and really no other place to go, they couldn't just retreat to the country to escape disease like many others did, including Robert Shields. They *were* the country. It was like retreating from themselves. They had to bloom where their seeds were sown. Besides, they couldn't just leave their fields and crops and animals to camp out somewhere else just because some typhoid was 60 miles away. No, not practical or feasible at all. And so, they stayed in place and warded off the evil spirits or decay or whatever it was, all on their own with their pine knots and chickens and lime and fires. With God's help of course.

Such faith was of little surprise, for the cove residents were deeply religious. Yet they also all had intensely realistic and practical veins running through their faithful bodies. The cove community was entirely dependent on nature; their lives were dictated by it. The weather, abundant animals, the creeks remaining full, the ebbs and flows of the environment, seasons, diseases, herbs, sunshine, rain, and food. All of this dependence had a direct effect on their ability to make a living, and their chances to survive. When Luraney and John were the only ones in the new wilderness, they prayed and worshipped within their own homes, prayed for food, health, and others. But now, with more and more families moving in, religion was taking a more central and formal role, and not just for praying that no typhoid came to visit with the poison dust lingering on their breath.

"Which worked, by the way," said Luraney to the group of women weeks later, when speaking of the power of prayer in the face of typhoid fever. "Because we never got an outbreak."

The women nodded. "Amen." They were sitting under the trees at the Oliver homestead, needles in hand, old scraps of clothing scattered on a stump, some very colorful and ready-made for quilting squares. Hands busy, they were all thankful for their healthy men, children and friends.

Luraney stopped sewing for a moment and closed her eyes, breathing in the freshest air she'd ever breathed. *God, look at how far we've come. And He said yes, look around.*

Surrounded by friends and what a large and healthy family you have! Thinking back to that first winter, pregnant.

Starving. The relief of receiving simple pieces of dried pumpkin from tall, red men who spoke a strange language. Jobe coming back, the only thing to look forward to were two milk cows ...pumpkins and cows. Neighbors arriving; her soap and butter...the hardest time in her entire life... She opened her eyes. *But look where I am now. Thank you, God.*

The eagle soared overhead. Luraney saw it and felt a sense of calm and resolve. Religion. Found within the trees, eagles, beasts, winds, and by her own fire in the evenings. Everyone needs peace and hope. *Wherever and however you find it.*

Luraney picked up an olive green and white checked square and placed it on her lap. Needles clicked as the eagle circled the quilting women.

God knew we didn't need any more trials.

"June 16, 1827! A great day for Cades Cove!" John cried out on a bright Saturday in front of the simple white building with smooth siding. It was not too large, but big enough to hold the rituals of weddings, funerals, and Sunday talks. But not baptisms, for the Baptist "theology had long been established with an abhorrence of infant baptism and an insistence on complete separation of church and state."

The very next day, Sunday, John Oliver acknowledged the initial congregation. "Thank you to all of you—all ten people who will establish the initial church membership." They finally had a church! Beyond the hearths of homes, beyond the meetings in the middle of the cove and away from the quilting circles under the trees with the eagles soaring overhead. The people now had a rock, a place where they could worship and grieve and celebrate.

John Oliver proudly listed them aloud, nodding and smiling to each: "Richard Davis, Preacher; William Davis, Clerk; myself and my wife, Luraney Oliver; James Oliver; James and Emily Johnson; Edward James; John Lacy and Christopher Winders."

John then ceremoniously announced that this new church was "an arm of the Wears Cove Church and that after prayer to God and his blessings, they choose Brothers Richard and Davis to lead us." The small crowd clapped their hands and bowed their heads in gratitude. Inside the church, there were no adornments. The light-colored planks of the floor blended up to the walls and to the ceiling. It appeared to the churchgoers as if they were inside a rectangular polished tree. Pews lined up in neat rows—only ten, five on each side. Up front and to the sides, six pews—three on each side—lined up facing the Communion table. They didn't believe in altars. Only a candlestick and a Bible adorned the table, but oftentimes, though lit, no candle was needed for light, for they had numerous windows to capture the rays of God.

That first Sunday held much excitement. *We have our own place of worship!* They kept repeating it, so thankful because they just couldn't quite believe it yet. Oh, they'd always had full faith and knew God would provide; actually, they would communicate with God anywhere. But a dedicated place to meet and worship meant everything. The Olivers had been here almost a decade and this was the very first church built in the cove. The sense of accomplishment and glory and permanence were palpable.

We did it!

Finally.

Our men built this holiest of places with their bare hands. Thank you to our husbands, sons, brothers, fathers, and uncles. Those ladders they built to get to the roof. Reining their horses to fell the best of trees. Clearing space for our loved ones who pass, right under the largest and broadest of chestnut trees. The one whose leafy shadows provide permanent lacy layers below. Building a perfect vessel for God; Jesus Christ himself began this church and it was perfect from the start.

God be praised.

An isolated community of farmers had created more than a church; it was a hub, a place to gather, share stories, practice their religion, and get news from their neighbors. It was almost like a seat of government. Those planks of wood, built with care in the shape of a simple rectangle with a steeple reaching to the sky, would now bear witness to the crisscrossing of happiness, sadness, celebrations, births, deaths, and rhythm of life of the Olivers and their neighbors.

Richard Davis would serve as the actual Preacher, but that day, John Oliver held the roles of both clergyman and court over his community and neighbors. The Preacher felt the tiniest twinge of disconcerting emotion at John receiving attention from one and all. But the Preacher was new to this community and knew John was the most decent of men. While settling into his humble cabin this past week, he'd heard some neighbors—admittedly only one or two who seemed kind of gruff anyway—that lamented that nothing could be done without the consent of John Oliver. Watching him hold court that day though, the Preacher soon melted at the character and integrity—the utter fairness—of the man who was here first. The bully, Tipton's son, always says things that are not entirely true or nice anyway. Especially to newcomers who he could get to first. Oh sure, Jake had calmed down enough—no more fighting, but there was always a certain gruffness, that wily undercurrent that ran through his veins... He vowed to keep an eye on him.

But on that first Sunday, the small wood building standing tall in the middle of a clearing, the land beside it cleared and tamped down for their cemetery, not one person complained that there could be nothing done within the cove without the Oliver family. Instead, the Preacher observed that the inhabitants, one and all, stood in line to thank and bless the head of the first family of Cades Cove.

As each parishioner shook John's hand and the group made its way outside to the bright sunshine, they were greeted with the especially large and strong eagle descending down and landing on the steeple.

By 1828—not even a full year into the new church, there was a fracture between the people in regard to their religion. The smallest scars within a belief system fester until they become a gangrenous fuel of broken faith.

"What's that famous sayin'? Oh yes, that lighthouses are more helpful than churches!"

John sighed upon hearing Jobe's words. He recognized his hero, Ben Franklin's words; though he preferred the other side of the issue which he could almost recite by heart: "Here is my Creed. I believe in one God, creator of the Universe. He governs it by His Providence. And ought to be worshipped. That the most acceptable service we render Him is doing good to his other children. The soul of Man is immortal, and will be treated with justice in another life respecting its conduct in this." Being Baptist, he believed the Bible was life's only reliable guide. But John was also practical, as was Ben Franklin; though their lives were lived many decades apart, both men recognized and knew that religion bound and divided people in the best and worst ways.

"Why *should* we support missions?"

"Agreed. It's not authorized in the Scriptures!"

"Besides, won't our money be best used here? We need to survive! We only got a bit over ten people now ...."

"Take care of our own first. That's what we need to do. And stick to the Bible. It tells us all we need to know. No messin' with it."

And on the other side: "We need Sunday schools ...no harm in testing our fellowship."

"The Bible indicates mandatory missions. They are not optional ...we need to share our gospel with one and all ...help with the health of our community. And even beyond."

The conversation grew heated; there was much-fueled talk every Sunday, every Wednesday in the middle of the fields, every Friday and Saturday night in rocking chairs by the many hearths of the cove. Inevitably, there was a permanent split in thinking, in priorities. *Religion divides people better than it brings them together.* John knew this was paraphrased heavily from Franklin and others but had to admit its truth. *But I'm stickin' to my principles and my God.*

This split in priorities divided the cohesiveness of thought, and thus, resulted in a split in loyalty to the lone church of the mountain valley. Surprising it was that all these pioneers, ever intent on nature and survival, made such a fuss about religion; such agitation was testament to the importance of faith, hope, and strength in this wild world. But when things in human lives are going well, whenever there is plenty of food, crops growing, children being born, and community cohesiveness, people start having more time on their hands. They begin thinking. And that thinking leads to questioning and contradicting.

"This is such a difference of opinion ...perhaps we need to build our own church ...."

"We want to do things differently. And they won't let us."

"They'll never let us. Lording their way over us."

"We should make our own...other towns have many churches. We should too."

"We have the land ...."

"We have the will ...."

"We have a plan ...."

John and Luraney Oliver, the Jobes, Tiptons, and the Shields family were all prosperous, doing well, expanding their families and farms, and co-mingled family and business. Being poor in money never mattered, for they were rich in land and food and family. Alas, nothing stays the same and life's calm heights never exist without the dips of worries and crises. One that hadn't reared its head in some time, yet grew in its intensity to now come to a head, was the matter of the Indians.

1838 blew in with wicked winter storms. Men, women, and children stayed indoors, save for necessary chores: milking the cows, tending the animals, gathering more wood from the immense pile stacked by the house, and general repairs. It was so cold that John stomped into the house every 20 minutes to warm up. "I'm bound to get frostbite out there!" He couldn't recall a winter so brutal. *Except maybe the first one.* Thank goodness, Luraney had a hot stew or soup over the hearth at all times. And coffee.

When an early spring finally came, he could hardly remember what it felt like to be comfortable. The warmer breezes, the ability to shed some layers, were welcomed more than anything he could recently think of. He never forgot that first brutal winter when it was so frigid and they were starving; the Indians had saved their lives. But it was these very Indians that he would have to soon round up and expel from this land. Their land.

Spring appeared in all its splendor, holding in its hands the expectation of births, hope, Lent and Easter, and an abundance of seeds to plant for harvest that is soon to come. Hope did not extend to the Indians, however. It was 1838, and the Indians had been here ...well, they didn't really know how long, but they knew that it was long enough to have seen the Spaniard Hernando De Soto in the 1500s. Before Shakespeare, Wordsworth and Newton. Before Galileo saw his moons of Jupiter through his telescope. Way before the 1630s establishment of the Massachusetts Bay Colony in America. The Taj Mahal hadn't been dreamed of, much less completed. And the Enlightenment and further tolerance were still far, far, away.

"The ones who were here first..." the men frowned. They didn't want to think of the Indians like that, even though it was true. They wanted to feel like they discovered this land, and that the land was waiting for them. Including the gold.

"They need to go west of the Mississippi. It's our gold. And it's what Jackson wants." the men stated to one another. Justification. Historical events could *always* be justified.

As Jobe constantly stated; he being a huge fan of repetition, "We're the ones that cultivated this land! We built, planted, and made our homes here. They never lived here. Never planted a full and ongoing crop. Never lived here at all, or built even one home."

Tipton agreed. "Besides, we can grow our community without the threat of Indian fighting or interference. We are just two different types. They'll be better off out west. They don't use gold anyway. That's solely a white man's currency."

"The gold *was* found on their lands..." one of the women ventured, but immediately regretted her voicing her opinion.

"Their lands? *Their* lands?! Who goes out every morning and tends the fields? Who built a church on sacred soil? For goodness sake, some of our people are buried here!" Tipton was furious at the notion that this land wasn't uniquely theirs. "Trust us. They'll be better off."

That year of 1838, when spring came in like nature extending its hand, saw the removal of fourteen thousand Cherokees. President Van Buren and his General Winfield Scott's 7,000 troops made sure of it. It took until late summer and even into fall and winter to remove these Indians, but when they did, the United States Army marched them—all of them; men, women and children—westward. Bayonet points at their very backs.

The race of red men was in despair, cold with the coming winter, and weary from the journey. Disease added to the misery. Imagine being forced from your home! The land where your ancestors roamed and spirits hovered over, forever protecting. The land you knew so well. The herbs of the mountains, the medicines, trees, and bushes that could be used for health and wellness. How to locate and track the game of the area; they knew migration routes, secret tracks, dens, and nests. Every peak, tree, rock outcropping, and creek were familiar landmarks, taught by the elders to the young ones from the earliest of ages. Nobody ever got lost. At least not accidentally.

Less than ten thousand Cherokee made it to the Indian Territory, west of the Mississippi.

The ones that made it told their sad tales around each and every campfire, every single night, for decades to come.

"We survived the Trail of Tears," the Chief began each and every night.

"Nunna daul Tsuny."

The Trail where they cried.

"And that nice white man. His name was John Oliver." The Chief continued. "We saved his life. And his wife. She was always so scared." he bowed his head, sad.

"Imagine our surprise when he showed up with the local militia—he had been part of the fighters, their Army, once, a long time ago ...he showed up, tasked with the final roundup of our people. John Oliver ..." he shook his head, his voice breaking. He silently wondered why ...for the thousandth time. No answer ever came to him.

"We saved his life." And in the flickering firelight that evening, the Chief felt the spirit of a teachable moment to the young and weary of his group. The fresh and worn faces looked at him with heavy mixtures of grief and anger. But he knew what he had to teach them; the hardest lesson of all. "It was the right thing to do. And we would do it again."

There were some who defied the order to walk all the way west. They hid in the mountains and migrated elsewhere. Hearty people, they no doubt knew exactly where to go to hide. Rare was the sighting of a Cherokee in Cades Cove after 1838.

ᘓᗉᗇChapter Sixᗇᘚᗉ

1840s

When things are going well, whenever there is plenty of food, crops growing, children being born, and community cohesiveness, people start having more time on their hands. They begin thinking. And that thinking leads to questioning and contradicting.

"This is such a difference of opinion ...perhaps we need to build our own church...."

"We want to do things differently. And they won't let us."

"They'll never let us. Lording their way over us."

"We should make our own ...other towns have many churches. We should too."

"We have the land...."

"We have the will...."

"We have a plan...."

It took until May 15, 1841, another fine spring day where Nature's heated hand extended in welcome. Why do human differences always seem to reach a breaking point right when nature is in the process of building anew? The cove community was still prospering, but the rise in population resulted in just a few too many differing minds to appease. Men find two ways to deal with injustice: to show it plainly or to hide all traces of it. Of course, Greeks thought an insolvable crisis could be solved by a combination of their many Gods getting involved. But no God would intervene and save the hero here.

The Missionary Baptist Church was organized—actually forced—over such minor and major disputes as Sunday School -*where in the Bible was that requirement?*- the Primitive Baptists hollered. *If they didn't go to school on Sundays, weren't they still doing God's work*, the old-school yelled? *Missionary work ...they really should conduct missions of God's work, shouldn't they?* Those who were anti-missionary were now dubbed Primitive Baptists—like John and Luraney. Those who said there doesn't need to be Sunday school were Primitives—the word meaning more than just basic level thinking. They were old-fashioned, set in their ways, and *certainly not dedicated to the true work of God,* they yelled back.

It could not be smoothed over, no compromise could happen. And so, thirteen members of the original church were excluded. Immediately, they formed their own—the Missionary Baptist Church. "We will innovate our beliefs to include missions and missionary work."

"We'll be officially known, from now on, as the Primitive Baptist Church." Oliver and the remaining members stated. "We will stick to the word of God. What's in the Bible. And if it don't say it, we don't follow it."

The growing cove community now had two churches.

This time, the mighty Olivers had no part in the new church. For once, something could be done without the Olivers having their hand in it. But that was factually incorrect, for the first family's presence was felt nonetheless. Always full of grace, character, and neighborly spirit, John and Luraney Oliver showed complete acceptance even though they did not share in the others' beliefs. Every successful community, especially a small, isolated mountain circle of homesteads and farms, needed a leader of peace. John embodied that role, continuously offering assistance—it wasn't taken; but just the fact that it was offered is testament to how respected and respectful he was. John was saddened by the split; however, he thought about the Indians and his friends and neighbors, and how they allowed each other to simply live and let live ...for the most part. Wasn't that the path to tolerance?

What did *live and let live* really mean to the Cades Cove humans? *Work decently, honestly, let everyone live the way they want as long as they don't hurt anyone else, mind your own business, make choices that didn't hurt others...* But doesn't that make us vulnerable? What if we think someone is acting irresponsibly, dangerously, or immorally? Do we simply just let those people live how they want? How about when they touch our own community, their base tendrils reaching around to embrace our children without them even knowing it?

And why did some in the cove think so differently given they all lived in the same place, under pretty much identical circumstances? They all planted, toiled the fields, hunted, tended animals, raised children, ate, slept, watched the eagles soar above their homes.

Luraney tried to make her husband laugh. "I don't know how it happens, but I meet with nobody but myself that is *always* in the right." She had just quoted Ben Franklin, and John recognized it with a chuckle, grateful for the release.

"I see what you mean, Luraney. Everyone thinks they are the only ones who are right."

"Aren't I though?" she teased.

John smiled. But with lingering sadness, he watched as his own people who had once embraced that live and let live way of thinking *together*, just couldn't do that anymore. It was now, live and let live, *but only if you agree with me.*

And, deeper and deeper in thought, John suddenly realized: *this splitting of perceptions was not only escalating towards our own, but talk had recently sped up regarding the Indians and some hushed regret about the fact that they'd pushed them off their own land. Together, but separate. Live and let live.*

"I just hope we all don't grow too far apart and a semblance of peace can last." John whispered to his wife as they fell asleep that night in their comfortable bed.

"For us? Or for us and the Indians?"

"Both, if I'm being honest."

It was a moment or two before Luraney answered. "It won't."

Despite the religious split, John Oliver remained destined to cross through every happening in the mountain valley community he had founded. But there was still the presence of the original residents of the cove—Indians—now seen less and less often, yet talked about more and more.

The remaining Indians who hadn't been pushed along the Trail of Tears, who peered through the brush to look at the white men in front of their wood-planked buildings who prayed and sang songs, couldn't quite put their finger on why or what the white man disputes were. After all, spirits were all around, and after all, everyone on earth was part of the "A ni yun wi yah" -*The Principle People, The People of God.* So what was the problem? The Indians discussed this in their campsites but never could reach an answer other than *people were always trying to do their own new thing when the original way is usually the best.* To the Indian culture, their "devotion was to the Supreme Holy Spirit, who could not be looked upon and whose energy was the fire of all creation and the fire of all life."

The Chief explained to his people, especially the young ones, who were in constant wonder about the white men. "Our Spirit resides in the heavens and on earth through purified people." The Indians were non-idolators; not observing any religious images or idolatrous religious ceremonies.

"There is one great spirit for the Cherokees—God, who is the only Giver and Taker of life."

The Chief continued, his lined and experienced face serious and somber above the light of the campfire. "We are all devoted to a higher principled way of living according to our ancient religious beliefs of the one benevolent God." When their story was told, which was told late into the night on a Saturday evening, they all vowed to walk near the settled part of the cove in the morning to peer some more at the white man's ways. Races, tribes and civilizations are in constant struggle to understand one another. Each comes across as something that we may not intend. Misunderstandings, underestimations, yes. But mostly it's that we all think we are nicely illustrated to others, in the same ways we see ourselves.

The red and brown men looked at each other when the pale ones walked out of the crude, but neat steepled building on Sunday, talking amongst one another. The ladies were in dresses; all carried rather large leather books. The children all in shoes. Men wore clean shirts and pants.

The Indians were far enough away that no churchgoing man would sense their presence. Still, they recognized figures. *There's that Oliver family. So many of them now! John— a good man.*

"We bow to no man. We kiss no idol. This is God's direct instruction." said the Indian with the highest status. He wanted to be sure that the young knew their special place in their world, all the while shielding them from the realities of this fast-moving dynamic between the two peoples.

The churchgoers lingered, talking amongst themselves. Laughing, whispering ...the children ran off with their country-fed energy. Some sat on quilts under the largest and broadest of chestnut trees, sharing and eating their food.

Looking at each other, the Indians raised eyebrows, the high status Indian suddenly jerked his head as if to say, "Let's go," and they all followed, went on their way to hunt for food and to worship in their own way.

High clouds and blue sky welcomed their hunt and the result was bountiful. Six deer! They'd even seen the eagle, but it was so far away.

All the rest of that afternoon, even through the hunt, the high-status Indian thought about their observation of the church and felt uneasy. Even a bit ominous. They were so different, these two peoples. Yet, here they were; they had shared an area of land in relative peace save for the occasional encounter for years. Then, the white man threatened and pushed them out. But his small band of defiant survivors remained here, hidden from any tracking methods they could come up with. For his people were one with this earth. Memories of his ancestors passed through his own thoughts and very body. The pale ones would never find them. But now, as the months of hiding took their toll, he wondered whether this state of affairs could continue. And if he was honest with himself, he already knew it couldn't. His wise soul filled with sadness, anger, and resolve. Because all he could do at the moment, breathing in the fresh mountain air and viewing the soft beauty of the basin, was walk away and join his own because he knew in his heart that this was what God wanted.

The age of pioneering was in the rearview mirror and the Industrial Age managed to arrive in the cove of Tennessee in the form of the Cades Cove Bloomery Forge. Medieval times were responsible for humanity's process of smelting iron from its oxides making for a mixture that was used to make wrought iron. Knives, sword blades, and other such ironworks were now possible, and this possibility arrived with yet another new resident, Daniel Foute.

"Daniel Foute built it," the residents conversed amongst themselves, and marveled at the beginnings of the "Single most important entrepreneur of the cove." Foute was quickly accumulating land in the surrounding areas and inside the cove itself and would, in fact, become a major landholder.

"He came from Greene County, and he's hooked in with Robert Shields."

"Isn't he also hooked in with David Emmett? David helped build the forge didn't he?"

"Yes, I think that's 'bout right."

The residents spoke of Foute from time to time, marveling at his can-do spirit. They all possessed it in some form of specialty, but Foute seemed to possess it when it came to technology, progressiveness… In many things, the cove residents weren't as forward-thinking as others in the bigger towns. They simply didn't see the need. *Wasn't the way we did things good enough? Didn't it work?* The thing is, they were right—things *did* work. And so, the collective thinking was, there was no necessity to change.

Foute, though, kept on going. Literally. He kept the cove moving and connected. Horse trails were rural roads, to and from other places. And Foute wanted the isolated cove to be connected. He made wider, smoother horse trails, or roads, and opened up thoroughfares from Happy Valley to Cades Cove, and from Cades Cove to Parson's Turnpike through Chestnut Flats. Horses and wagons could now travel easier and faster.

Trade increased and the cove was busier.

"But he still doesn't live here himself!" the Olivers, Jobes, Tiptons and Shields families lamented over and over again. *Why have such a stake if it doesn't even affect you directly?* They couldn't understand it. For them, their lives were tied to the land. And they loved their land like it was a limb on their bodies. They did not differentiate between their own bodies and the body of the earth.

It wasn't until 1848 that Foute himself moved into the cove to "take over a more active management of his properties." Active would describe the entirety of the cove at that time, because by the mid-Century year of 1850, the population of Cades Cove was a robust 685, full of happy, content, active people, complete with schools, churches, homesteads, and a forge.

"In fact," William Tipton told Joshua Jobe and John Oliver one day while crossing paths in between their homesteads, "That noise his forge makes is too much for the wolves."

"What do you mean?" asked John.

"What I mean is the wolves were so scared by the noise, they done left the day it opened."

"Wait, I've seen wolves after it opened!" Jobe argued.

"No." said John. "Never really thought on it before. But Bill's right. Think on it. Ne'er seen wolves again."

"And you won't. They can't take the noise."

He *was* right. The residents loved this side effect of the forge. Not only did they have access to wrought iron, the wolves who were a "dangerous and often threatening symbol of their wilderness experience finally ended." But not everyone was happy. The Cherokees, though seen the very rare time these days, revered the wolf, seeing the animals as watchdogs and hunters, and associating the animal with courage, loyalty and strength. They even had a special "teaching story" about the wolf that every one of their young hunters and huntresses learned:

An old Cherokee is teaching his grandson about life. "A fight is going on inside me," he said to the boy. "It is a terrible fight and it is between two wolves. One is evil. He is anger, envy, sorrow, regret, greed, arrogance, self-pity, guilt, resentment, inferiority, lies, false pride, superiority, and ego."

He continued, "The other is good. He is joy, peace, love, hope, serenity, humility, kindness, benevolence, empathy, generosity, truth, compassion, and faith. The same fight is going on inside you – and inside every other person, too."

The grandson thought about it for a minute and then asked his grandfather, "Which wolf will win?"

The old Cherokee simply replied, "The one you feed.

"Well, the wolves are banished ...can we hope that the rest of the Indians will be too?"

"What?" John shocked them all by his reaction, he being one of the ones who expelled them from their land. He being the one whose life was saved by them. "But some of them work for you ...right there in your forge!"

"Yep, they do, John. The ones who didn't move west. When we *asked* them to." he huffed, then continued. "Yessir, they're good workers. But like the wolves, there may be no place for them here anymore. Perhaps their time has come and it's goin' quickly. Maybe it's gone already."

"Like the wolves." repeated the men, in unison, while nodding and bowing their heads.

Photo Gallery

Photographer:

Dean Alexander Astl

JOHN OLIVER CABIN

JOHN OLIVER CABIN – FRONT VIEW

JOHN OLIVER CABIN

THE CANTILEVER BARN

INSIDE THE CANTILEVER BARN

REBECCA (AUNT BECKY) CABLE'S HOUSE.

METHODIST CHURCH

PRIMITIVE BAPTIST CHURCH

INTERIOR OF THE MISSIONARY BAPTIST CHURCH

INTERIOR OF THE PRIMITIVE BAPTIST CHURCH

INTERIOR OF THE METHODIST CHURCH

JOHN CABLE MILL

CADES COVE

ABRAMS CREEK

JOHN AND LURANEY OLIVER'S GRAVE AT THE PRIMITIVE
BAPTIST CHURCH.

RUSSELL GREGORY'S GRAVE AT THE PRIMITIVE BAPTIST
CHURCH.

MARTHA OLIVER'S GRAVE AT THE PRIMITIVE BAPTIST CHURCH. MARTHA WAS THE FIRST OLIVER BORN IN THE COVE.

REBECCA CABLES GRAVE AT THE CABLE CEMETERY.

MARTHA "POLLY" OLIVER'S GRAVE THE PRIMITIVE BAPTIST
CHURCH.

ᚈᚱ᚜Chapter Sevenᚲᚳᚷ

1830s-1840s—Part II

By now, the Oliver family boasted two more children—Ruth, born back in 1833, and William M. Oliver, or Bill as they called him, in 1837, bringing the total Olivers in the cove to nine: John and Luraney, and Polly, Martha, Elizabeth, Lazarus, Elijah, Ruth and William.

"It's like a roll call!" John happily exclaimed every night when playfully counting his robust family.

John Oliver, the patriarch of Cades Cove, was now forty-four years old. His wife was forty-two—both still extremely sturdy at a time when the average life expectancy hovered around the forty to fifty-year-old mark. They felt better than ever; the fresh air of the mountains, and hard, but noble work, contributing to their longevity.

The years went on, seasons came and went, crops thrived almost every season. There were some leaner years. But nothing like that first winter. *Nothing would be like that first winter. Because they had each other. We will get through it. As a community. As a family. One and all. Would you like some butter? My cows are producing. Yes, thank you, and I have some ham we can spare ...will you take some for tonight? Cook it up for all those youngin's you have? God bless you and your family. Thank goodness for our neighbors! Luraney, can I get some of that honey soap? Perhaps with walnuts? It sure takes the grime right off! I'll swap you some calico for the girls' dresses.* And one and all clamored for her pumpkin butter.

They all praised and prayed by their hearths at night, thankful that they had help in this wild, wild place they called home. One and all knew they'd never be able to exist alone. As a result of this neighborly, friendly and helpful way of living, the Cades Cove community survived and thrived. The years meandered on, children were born, people passed, the eagle continued to soar—it was the offspring of the original of course, they only lived about twenty years, but an eagle was always soaring and swooping through the cove, watching the humans walk up and down nice and neat rows of crops, the females with eggs in their bellies, while they themselves flew back to their nests at night to incubate their own eggs. The residents always stopped to look up at them—the majestic eagle, it was always there. Even now, through America's, and the cove's, 1830s, '40s and '50s eras.

Other places in the United States of America enjoyed the Second Great Awakening and the invention of the mechanical reaper; U.S. citizens interested in happenings across the pond saw the rise of Queen Victoria in England and watched the rise of colonialism and imperialism. At home, President Andrew Jackson, "Old Hickory," became the people's President and was working to found the Democratic Party, working his Hermitage plantation, and using the power of the veto pen for the first time in Presidential history.

The Cades Cove Community lived a bit differently.

The population hovered at seventy households and 450 men, women and children, but those numbers were rising quickly. Privacy in these frontier homes was rare, but people managed to keep on having children and they were always welcomed. As ever, more people meant more help on the homestead and farm. More people in a humble log cabin also led to some changes in where to fit everyone. Parents and infants and daughters slept on the first floor and sons on the second floor in the lofts of the simple log homes. Life centered in the main room downstairs; older folks lived with families too, and "a headcount of ten to twelve under one roof was not unusual."

Housing improved. Early on, construction was hasty, with very little hewing and many knots and stubs remaining. Clay was flung into holes and allowed to dry. It didn't look very polished. Within a few years though, being better established and adapted to the cove, residents took much more care in choice and use of materials, with corner notching of a more durable type and executed much better than before. Made for a much tighter fit; better insulated from the elements.

Of course, John Oliver had no help at all save for his own two hands and grit when he made his first rough cabin during that first approaching winter; these later years proved easier with increased help, better tools, and more knowledge of what worked and what didn't. More homes were made from split logs, bigger and flatter stones were placed in each corner for a solid foundation, and some professions advertised who they were by the way their house was built. Peg holes in the logs on the porch told one and all that a weaver lived there; his wares hung for all to see. *Smoke from thousands of fires clung to kitchen walls after a time*...all mixing together to fill the air with aromas of stews, lighting the evenings of children and men alike, and providing sustaining warmth for the people of the cove through many harsh winters.

128

Furnishings for the homes were also more abundant, now that the Oliver family had more hands on the farm from its own large family, and therefore more time for improvements. Their cabin boasted a small bed for both he and Luraney, and one each for the children in the loft, heavy and loving quilts covering each one. A table and a few chairs and sturdy stools rounded out the small log cabin. Quilts could be spread anywhere—even on floors—for the clan to sit upon, while they were inside. Truth be told though, most activities of daily living were outside the cabin, the door open most of the time to infuse continuous fresh mountain air—it could get awfully smoky and stuffy inside.

Like all pioneer women, Luraney worked hard, multiple times a day just to keep a clean house. *Constant sweeping I'm doin'! And moppin'!* Her most lathery soap and 'elbow grease' was spread all over the floors, *so clean we can eat off of them.* Indeed, every few months, John had to make her another broom and mop, the old ones becoming crumbly and as dirty as the barn floor. The children loved throwing the old brooms into the fire—it made for a wide and sputtering bombardment right inside in the hearth. But no matter the constant labor to keep their wood-planked floors clean, it was better than hard-packed dirt floors, or the inside of a wagon. And she had to admit, the cabin was well-built, well-insulated with mud and moss and such filling in all cracks. When it rained it got damp inside to a degree, but not as bad as other folks' homes, some of whom had downright waterfalls streaming down walls during heavy downpours.

Yes, we're mighty proud of our home, they'd compliment each other at night when they thought the kids were asleep. *Pride in one's home ...that is what I was seeking when I came here. My own farm. My own home. We did it, Luraney.*

Home. The tiny strong log cabin tucked away amongst the trees rested itself with the family's soft nighttime breaths. It too slept away the night covered with the warm and colorful quilts, clothes and their many work rags hanging by the fireplace at night, readying for the next day's labor.

During the 1830s, '40s, and beyond, the Oliver family was thriving. Two of John and Luraney's daughters married into the Shields Family—Polly marrying Henry Frederick, and Martha married to Henry Harrison, and everyone was busy working the fields, gathering for dinner in the evenings, sleeping well with sound and fulfilling thoughts, and attending church on Sundays and Wednesdays. Weddings were a big deal in the cove, but Luraney's daughters opted, as was becoming the custom, to have their ceremonies in the family home rather than in the church.

"We can't have the happy juice in the church," Polly Oliver whispered to her friends when asked about her decision not to get married in the church. "Elizabeth feels the same way. And to be sure, our Henrys *definitely* agree!" The girls laughed, nodding their heads.

"But we can have all we want at home! The one time our parents let us have four sips and never say a word."

"Speaking of home—you know the boys'll raid the house, grabbing the groom and paradin' him around the house!" her friend answered, speaking loudly now so the young men could hear. "Oh yes, that's their tradition. Silly, but boys ...they all act like they're sittin' on the highest corn when one of 'em is marrying." The young men walked around in mock strutting, causing the girls to roll their eyes, but heartily laugh.

"Y'all going to live on the homestead right?" One of the local young women wanted to know if her friend was following the custom of leaving the original nest, only to go to the one right next door. "Yep, we got a weaner house ...ha! I bet you boys love what we call that!" She directed her statement towards the young men, who, true to form, bawdily teased the young ladies about the "weaner house."

"Well, y'all will love that tradition! You'll see. Tease on it all you want! But makes all the sense. See, we can be alone in our first days of marriage, but at the same time, we have all the help we could need—the folks bein' right next door."

"Or at least close by. How we gonna keep our very first homes and our very first farms all at once? Our parents learned, now it's our turn, and someday..." they smiled at the girls, "we are going to teach our own kids."

When one of them was getting married, they'd always get together in a group under the Oliver homestead trees, for they were especially thick and cool, and they would reminisce about their shared cove childhood. It was a solid tradition. And since they married into each other's families—*who else was available? Certainly not anyone from Chestnut Flats!* - their companion memories would be the foundation that would bond them to each other until they had time to create and add brand new ones. Usually married by the age of twenty, twenty-two years old or so, they all had a lot of memories to go over.

"Remember attending school? It wasn't so bad. And we did learn a lot—at least as much or more than those fancy northern schools."

"But we walked so long to school! Four miles!" the boys whined. "They'd let us out so late too ...4:00 p.m. most days! Then, home, chores, studyin', Dad would read to us from the Bible, and then bed for the night. That sun would slip behind those peaks with amazing quickness. So, to *reiterate*—

remember that nice formal word we was taught? Risin' early, all that work, then bedtime. Only to rewind it all over again."

"Well, school was alright. They really did teach us good ...excuse me, *well,"* The young man chuckled at his impression of the reading and writing teacher who had branded his memory with 'it's not that you're doing *good*, but doing *well*- that's the proper way to say it.'" He continued. "Lord, I will never forget that."

"You just did!" the girls ribbed.

"Ha ha! I was just makin' my point!" As the group of girls rolled their eyes. "School was good. They taught us *well*. He winked at his own wit. "But hear me ...I loved late November. That was my favorite. Hog-killin' time. They wouldn't let us around too much, being too young and all and so much blood they said, but them bladders..."

"Oh, I remember! That epic kickball game ...must've lasted all winter, even in the snow."

"We'd blow them up like balloons ...they'd never burst either."

They all laughed at the shared recollections of the pig bladder balloons being bounced and kicked around the entire perimeter of the cove. All the mothers yelled for us to "stop traipsing over our gardens retrievin' that ball! But they secretly loved us being busy and outta trouble."

"We'll probably be the same with our kids. We all seem to have so many 'round here."

"Well, pig bladders were fun. But ...my memories take me back to playin' in the creeks, always in the creeks. Remember we all were so proud when we hunted game too? Hopped right outta that creek and caught my first rabbit." They laughed. It may have been small game, but they still were entirely proud to have made that contribution to their families.

"You could catch a squirrel quicker'n green grass through a goose!"

"I recall the best times were gatherin' nuts and berries. Helping with harvests ...."

"Corn harvesting was the best time. Soon as the frosts came. See? That's what we need from our fathers while in our weanin' houses—how to harvest corn. Oh sure, we'd done it. Our whole lives in fact. But we only helped. Have we done it for an *entire* field? Not I. Not yet. You gotta cut it off right above the ear, stack 'em all up, tie 'em in a bundle ...tops and fodder gathered for the stock—cows, horses. Dry the corn then tossed into the wagon and pitched right into the corncrib. Mama—and soon our wives—would finally make the best grits, hominy ...man, it would stick to the ribs!"

"And Polly and Elizabeth—your mother's butter and pumpkin butter would be just the thing to make any biscuit or cornbread sent straight from Heaven."

"Yessir. And ma'ams," the young men grinned to the girls. All agreed that Luraney Oliver's butters had to be the best in the world.

"Helping with harvests ...yes. That is my favorite memory..." Henry Shields took the wet piece of hay from between his teeth and looked out over the fields. Everywhere he looked, the corn was high, golden; the husks holding yellow oblong scales of beauty.

"I agree." Polly Oliver, his future bride smiled at him, slipping her arm through his. "Those were the most festive times."

Polly watched her sister and Henry walk into a thick stand of trees. She took the arm of her own Henry ...they'd have to devise a way of keeping their two husbands with the same names straight! Their father sure liked the name Henry Shields, the only difference being their middle names. *Why was that?* They wondered out loud.

"Well, namin' a kid after a daddy is popular the world over. I think pretty much forever, it's been done."

"It was what kings called fealty ...remember we learned about them kings of England in school? When they taught history class? It means the kid will be more loyal to the family. Keeps 'em in line, waiting their turn, and not poisonin' their daddy to get to the throne."

"So namin' sons the same names keeps them waiting happily until it's their own turn eh?"

"Yes, but they always know that their turn will come."

"How 'bout that."

"And here, we talk about weaner houses and all that ...I guess we all have to wait our turn."

The others stood in thought, watching their friends, Polly and Elizabeth Oliver, stride away with the Shields boys, readying for their weddings. But the group of young adults was still basking in their clear-eyed memories, not ready to let them go just yet. The sun was still high in the sky that day as they collectively thought backward in time.

For, it was truly a happy season when Cades Cove children would turn their faces to the sun which had warmed the golden crops, and duck under the trees for refreshingly cool respites from the summer humidity. It was a happy time when the smallest residents could roam free, wading in the creeks, skipping rocks, doing chores without complaint, sitting through church services so they could fill their souls and then their bellies with treats that were brought for picnicking on Sunday afternoons. It was fun to get together on those days; depending on the season, they ran, dipped into branches of the creeks—Tater Branch Creek was a local favorite.

"That summer at Tater when the boys grew up! Their voices were changing and we made fun of them!"

"Oh, they were so mad!" The girls laughed, appreciating their hard, but happy upbringing. "But they didn't want to get out of that water to chase us!" They laughed, recalling vividly that hottest of summer days when the only relief that could be found was by submerging in the rocky creeks, always cold from winter's icy runoffs.

"Remember that one berry stemming weekend? We all gathered at the church and spent all day pickin' off those dang stems, and our mamas canned and preserved them? They did that boilin' bath method that preserves food practically forever. That was the best canning in years!" They all agreed, reminiscing about their berry-stained faces. "We ate more than they canned!" If their mothers were listening just then, they would wholeheartedly confirm this fact.

"How about bean stringing? When those early beans are picked and prepared for dryin' or pickin' in the pod."

"Yeah…"

"And then the later crop—the seeds hulled out and stored for soup beans? My mama makes the best bean soup…"

"I like apple peeling…"

"Corn husking is the best! It's so satisfyin' to peel and peel, and reveal that glorious corn. So yummy …."

"And that cider afterward was the best ever. Remember? Our mamas allowed us all the cider we wanted, as long as the corn was taken care of."

Indeed, growing up in the cove's playground of simple pleasures, marrying, raising a family and working their own land was just about the best thing in the world. They loved it, one and all. Hard work, yes, but it was the only life they ever knew. The only one they could imagine.

"I always liked the scarecrow in the yard. So lonely, standing there in overalls and an old shirt! But it worked. Never saw a crow since…"

"Dad built the barn before we even had a house!" they all laughed, but nodded in acknowledgment of a farm's priorities.

"Aw heck, I'd rather sleep in the barn. Our house had so many cracks in it, in winter, I woke up with snow on my bed!"

"Aw heck, when it rains, we have a dang waterfall right onto our kitchen table. Mama's always gettin' on us men and boys to plug them up with some mud. We just ain't got to it yet."

"Y'all never get to it, unless we nag you to the ends of the mountains!" The girls admonished. The boys—the same ones they'd marry one day—stuck out their tongues to them and yelled "nag!"

The group took a break, breaking off from one another. Girls gossiped, talking about which boys they'd like to marry. The boys did the same. As close-knit groups do, they both found themselves following each other to the creek, cupping their hands for a drink. The boys washed their faces and poured water down the backs of their necks. Sunlight hit the rocks of the creek so heavily that rays could be seen pushing themselves through the yellow birch and hickory leaves.

Sufficiently rested the girls stood, wiped off their dresses, and walked back to the Oliver's stand of thick trees. The boys followed. When they had all resumed their spots beside the fence and under the shade which was always quickly made for in this heat, they were together again in their shared memories.

"The doves calling. That's my favorite sound."

"The best time is when the dogwoods bloom…"

And finally, "When that huge bird soars, I know it will all be okay. Eagles explore their world. Eagles bring us courage."

With Daniel Foute and his bloomery forge—a huge boon for the growing community—the entrepreneurial spirit spread and Shields came together with Foute and another neighbor, David Emmett. Together, they built the first overshot water-powered grist and flourmill in the cove.

Shields was an ambitious man, as were Foute and Emmett, and all three looked to make a name for themselves within their mountain community, each in their own specialty. For his part, Shields leaned towards community politics and affairs and was elected Justice of the Peace for his, the Sixteenth Civil District. "One of his first acts was to petition for a road from Tuckaleechee to Cades Cove."

After that success, he continued his quest, making sure the cove was connected to Happy Valley and the other suburbs, as well as many neighboring towns. These acts helped the economy of the cove and as always, especially with anything new, were the subject of much discussion amongst the residents.

"They think we are all so isolated and don't have a stake in the greater area, but we do!" the menfolk constantly complained. "Us folks here need to make sure Knoxville gets steamboats and railroads coming through. Or at least close by. For us, it will open up the world to our crops, livestock…"

"Luraney makes a great soap too. And that butter …Mmmm mmmm …the best around. Wonder if there's markets for our homemade goods and crafts straight from these mountains?"

"I would imagine so. We just need them to know about it."

"Thank goodness Shields represents us. That new road'll do us all good. Oth'wise, no one would even know we was out here!"

Of course, there was still nothing that could be done in the cove without John Oliver, who involved himself in what Shields petitioned, what Foute and his friends wanted to build, and in all matters of the cove. And he directed many of his thoughts and ideas, at this point in time, to the solid sounding board that was Peter Cable.

Peter had come to the cove way back in 1825, when he and his brother, Dan, purchased land. Dan did not wish to live there; he just wanted to invest, but Peter jumped at the chance and brought his wife, Catherine, to the carved mountain bowl.

"Catherine, I believe this is the place where I could die in peace." Similar sentiments felt by John Oliver were also felt by Peter Cable as he arrived and walked the area, looking for the best place to settle. Much less land was available now, and he had to walk much further than John Oliver ever had.

"Here is the largest white oak tree in this gorge ...this is it!" he excitedly decided then and there to build their cabin on this spot of land. It was tucked back in the trees and dry. He could already see the plowed fields of his neighbors, smelled their livestock, watched the aroma-filled smoke from their chimneys, and heard the whispering of the creek. The purest mountain air he'd ever breathed calmed him immensely. It took under fifteen minutes from the time he stepped down from his wagon and inhaled his first glimpses of the cove to exclaim to his wife, "I have found what it means to be home." *How familiar this man seems,* the eagle thought as the sturdy man jumped from the wooden wagon. The eagle's sharpest eye caught the gleam in the man's face. Recognition. *That man has just come home.*

The Cables were immediately active in the mountain valley community and had three children by 1830, all born healthy and hearty in their humble cabin in Cades Cove.

Peter Cable and John Oliver became fast friends, best friends in fact. Both men shared the same mindset on everything, including their desire for a religious place that was true to their beliefs. Such desire, as what happened previously between the Primitive Baptist Church and the Missionary Baptist Church, typically festers until a break occurs, one that is fueled by independence, like-mindedness, and the need to do things in a drastically different manner that just cannot abide the old way.

"We're *all* Methodists and Baptists!" John exclaimed.

"But the age of salvation ...they think it doesn't have to be twelve."

"Salvation is only possible when a child reaches the age of twelve!" John had grown up with this belief firmly ingrained in his psyche. It was in the Bible and that was inalterable just because man wanted some flexibility. It was impossible to change that view.

Peter agreed. "But the missionaries and their group, they just can't bide that. Why can't young children be saved, they say. Why they have to be twelve? It's not right, they're yellin'. Such men just switch up the Bible at their every whim!"

Little did the men know that the disagreement would result in yet another split of the church. But that formal fracture would be left to their sons; neither man would survive to see yet another break in their beloved church. The future of religion in the cove was left in God's hands and the men's descendants, but for now, the more practical matter of the mail still had to be delivered.

"The post office ...finally!"

"When did the mail get here?" asked one of the children, sitting on a fence one summer day when the dogwoods were blooming and the air was filled with the earthy smell of crops and animals and sweaty men and women working their fields and gardens.

"Oh let's see." Catherine Cable said, laughing. "I don't really have to scour my brain; I recall that day like it was yesterday, little one." She ruffled the boy's golden hair.

"Mmmm ...It was so important, that day...." Luraney answered.

They were taking a break at midday for a drink under the Oliver's stand of thick trees.

Catherine had arrived way back in 1825, but, "it was on a glorious early-summer Friday, June 28, 1833. Remember? We had all grown really loud in our attempts to correspond with friends, family, business associates, and the outside world."

"Yes," Luraney laughed. "We wouldn't let up 'til we got our mail on a regular basis!"

"We were loud for sure. Louder than a wind storm blowin' up." The little boy laughed at that. "That sure is loud!"

"Yes. But it worked."

Absolom Renfro was the first postmaster of Cades Cove, crossing through the area during that early-summer month of June back in 1833. He made sure that mail was delivered from Sevierville once a week and he soon realized he enjoyed the ride into the beautiful valley bowl surrounded by softly curved mountains. The people were friendly and sometimes had a piece of cornbread or slice of ham waiting for him. The people seemed to work extra hard and there were so many children bustling about! They were in constant motion, he noticed, as he meandered his horse on the road leading into the cove community. The littlest ones already milking cows, carrying tin buckets from the creek, lugging wood to the woodpiles, and picking food from the gardens. Sometimes, he'd see the older ones walking in a line, coming home from school, toting tin lunch buckets, and some were barefoot, walking along the soft pine needles.

Sometimes he would stop his horse on the horse road leading into the cove and take in the beauty of the place, almost always noticing that one lone eagle flew over the fertile basin. The bird obviously lived here too. The wingspan was huge; seemed to be curious, and appeared to consciously observe the humans buzzing around the rich land. Sometimes,

141

the bird would dive down, as if to greet him, then fly to perch on a nearby thick branch, watching. He loved those moments. Always taking just a minute or so to admire the pastoral and idyllic scene before him. No other place he'd traveled to had the same mystical feel of the cove. He'd close his eyes, soaking it in so at least a little bit of its magic coated his insides.

Finally, opening his eyes again to the freshest of views, he took his bugle and announced his presence. The eagle still perched on a branch high above, flinched at the sound. He remained there, watching. Curious.

The bugle announcing that the mail had reached the cove was welcomed by all, even seeing grown men and women run from the fields to the postmaster's house to receive their highly anticipated weekly letters and parcels. Sometimes they even arrived before Absolom did, before he could even dismount and hitch his horse! It did not take long for the women to embrace the outside world and all its offerings. They devoured mail-order catalogs and wrote and received letters from family and friends. *The Maryville Times* was particularly popular as it contained all the news needed to keep the isolated community in the know.

After a while, Absolom would send a delivery boy for some of the cove deliveries, especially when other routes opened up and he was stretched thinner than ever, trying to get mail to the growing population of this area of Tennessee. The delivery boys had a long way to go to get to the cove, about thirty-five miles, despite roads opening up and it becoming easier to travel, and so, a resident of Sevierville asked of the cove residents, "I would take it as a great favor if you will let my mail boy stay one night in each week with you, and if you will do so I will pay you at the rate of twenty dollars a year."

Of course, the neighborly spirit of the cove people resoundingly agreed and soon, the first families of the cove—the Olivers, Tiptons, and Jobes—and many others, on a rotating basis, welcomed the regular mail boy once a week, gave him food and a warm bed, and made him the very center of attention. For he didn't just bring the mail. He brought stories.

"The people out in West Tennessee, they got themselves a mechanical reaper, finally."

The children drew close to the mail boy to find out about the scary sounding machine.

"See, they have lots of cereals out in their crops. This thing reaps, or gathers—cuts, if you will—the crops when they're just perfect—at the ripest peak."

"That's amazing!" Little Elijah Oliver said at the time. His birth in 1829 had just preceded all these new technologies of the farm.

The mail boy gestured to move closer and whispered to the ladies. "They're also publishing that abolitionist newspaper outta Boston." He saw the women's' eyebrows rise just a tad. But he didn't want to offend; he was in the South, in the mountains of Tennessee after all. "If you're so inclined that is." he tilted his hat and left it at that.

"There is some other news." he began. These ladies were so thirsty for knowledge of the outside world! They were in much better shape as far as news these days, with the mail being delivered regularly, but they still yearned for any and all accounts of happenings beyond the gentle slopes of these peaks.

"The women, all over the place, they're forming letter writing groups. The women write letters to friends of friends and such, and they form this big circle-like group who exchange letters. Some women asked me to ask the Cades Cove women if y'all'd like to participate?"

Luraney was the first one who jumped off the fence at which she was half leaning, half sitting outside the postmaster's house. Inside was just too crowded.

"Oh, that's a lovely idea!" She couldn't write very well when she arrived in the cove, but now, she was much better. Without really speaking out about it, she'd sought out her children's school experiences. For years now, they'd been teaching her, coming home from school and reviewing vocabulary and reading assignments with her. She just had to show interest and her sons and daughters delighted in proudly sharing what they'd learned that day. Enthusiasm and active involvement are keys to shared knowledge. And now, a letter-writing club was another chance to practice and learn even more!

"Indeed! What do you think, Catherine? Ruthie?" She looked round the circle of women who were desperate for new diversions. "I am sure my Polly and Elizabeth would also join in." All nodded and exclaimed a great desire to correspond with others in Western Tennessee and maybe even beyond.

"I will write letters to all my friends and kin in Chattanooga!"

"Mine are all in Knoxville."

"I am sure they will all expand our circle and then, sooner or later, we can write to new people."

"Imagine if we began correspondin' with ladies in New York?"

Change did not come easy to such folk. They toiled on their farms and homesteads year in and year out, changed routines four times per year, and then, only with the seasons. But, something new like this, something that let them reach outside the fertile bowl for just a few moments, yet still allowed them to limit the outside coming in, was very enticing. Outside people were welcomed warmly, but always with skepticism and a bit of a dubious wonder, at least until they got to know them. But letters—those were harmless! If they didn't like someone in a letter, they just threw it in the fireplace.

"Can't do that with people!" Catherine Cable snapped her fingers in jest, and her irascible humor made them roar with laughter.

"Oh don't repeat that!" she pleaded to the mail boy. "Don't want them all thinkin' we're mean folk."

"Never!" he said, crossing his heart, still roaring with laughter at the boldness of these fiery and funny women living within the beautiful isolated arena of bountiful land.

They all laughed until their sides hurt. And then, of course, they had to ask for forgiveness and pray it all away.

⟨⟩Chapter Eight⟨⟩

1850

Letter writing had become a regular activity for the women and men of the cove over the next few decades; the women especially embraced it and they gathered a couple times a month to write letters together, trade information and news and gossip. Literacy rates stood at roughly twelve percent for the world, yet the women of the cove were largely literate—at least enough to read their Bibles and write of gossip, reports and accounts of events, and to place orders from mail-order catalogs.

It was also their chance to boast to friends and relatives in other parts of Tennessee and beyond about their blessed fates. There was just a little boasting because they were on the whole a humble people, but they couldn't help but think that their loved ones would want to know how they fared.

The average farm in the cove, now that it is approaching the mid-century year of 1850—can you believe it?—is an impressive and valuable 150-300 acres. We are so very blessed. At the same time, there are smaller farms too. Those farms of 100 acres or less make up about three-quarters of the cove. Luraney wrote to their distant relatives.

Distance never mattered to mountain families. Kin was kin, no matter if they ever met or not. No matter if they ever visited or had anything to do with day-to-day lives. Family was a tie that never unraveled.

"Tell them that Franklin quote ....." John walked into the cabin for lunch just then. The sun was still low—it was only 10:30 in the morning, but he was already famished. "That sun is lickin' me today." He sat down and took off his hat, fanning himself with it. Luraney handed him a cold drink.

"Who're you writing to? The family? Tell them guests, like fish, begin to smell after three days." He laughed at his humor at quoting the pithiest of sayings of his favorite historical hero.

"Ben Franklin again?" Luraney exasperated, but couldn't help herself and laughed too. "I will do no such thing, John! Besides, they'll never visit here. So there's no worry about seein' them."

"Or them smelling up the place." He winked at Luraney's eyes that threatened to bore a hole straight through him, grabbed a biscuit and some ham, and went back out onto the porch. She actually loved that he broke the monotony of their days with his humor. It wasn't often, to be sure, but it was a nice respite when he did. How uplifting it is to laugh! She smiled, sat back down in the chair that she moved right to the middle of the floor. That way, the breeze came through the open door and cooled everything in its path. Writing on a stout piece of cardboard for a desk, she bowed her head, continuing her letter.

Mules, muscles, simple tools, and neighborly help are all needed to fell the trees, get them to building sites (we use our horses too), and build the houses. Let me tell you how the men do it. Round logs are scored along their length with a felling ax, then hewn with a broad ax.

We have so many tools now! If John doesn't have one he needs, some other neighbor is bound to have one. Or, the menfolk simply make what they need, or else they go up to the forge to make it. Regarding homes and barns and such, once they have the tools, corners are notched and need no nails or pegs to hold them together. Open spaces between are then filled with mud to seal out the wind. The stone chimney—our kitchens are lifelines as you know—are held together with mud mortar.

She was careful in her writing, never a strong skill of hers, making it more formal, making sure she spelled everything right. She sat back, thinking for a moment. Just *being* here in her home. Suddenly, removing herself from the chair in the middle of the cabin, Luraney put her writing materials down and walked outside to where John was still sitting, resting before taking to the fields again. He had a piece of hay, picking his teeth with it, and had his eyes closed. "Just resting?" she asked.

"Yeah. Sun's hot today."

"It is." She agreed. "A nice, cool salad with dinner tonight?

"Sounds great."

She suddenly bent to kiss her husband. A rare show of affection, he was surprised.

"I love you, John. Thank you for bringing me here."

She straightened and looked out into the fields, a cow close to the fence, the creek murmuring softly. Golden rows of corn and wheat. The eagle was flying high in the sky.

John smiled, eyes still closed.

Luraney walked back inside and sat down in the cane-backed chair. The door remained open and the sweet air engulfed the home. Quiet. A house of respite.

What else did she want to say in her letter?

With such wonderful and solid building techniques, our homes are so solid, and these techniques—remember, they're so good they need no nails or pegs—are used to build "businesses, schools, hospitals and nursing homes" in other areas of the country. Of course, we don't need those. Our homes are our hospitals and nursing homes. Our Elizabeth and Ruth are especially gentle in their caregiving. But we do have schools. And they are sturdy, rigorous, and hold the precious future of Cades Cove.

The wagon road known as Cades Cove Road is now well-traveled, between the mail boy, relatives coming to visit, and folks trading for our good corn and oats and such. My soap, especially the cakes with honey and walnuts, and my butter are well-received. The pumpkin butter is a real favorite. People from all around ask for it! This road—the main access to Tuckaleechee—is watched by the children very closely! They have much desire for any news from the outside world. In fact, we worry all the time about losing our children to the outside world, the bigger towns. But we just want them to be happy. Some of them do fly the nest, just like eaglets here in the cove, and we just have to make their flight as educated and experienced and well-bred as possible. But since the mail came to the cove, these youngins keep their eyes peeled for any glimpse of a wagon or horse! I dare say, one cannot get within three miles of the cove without one of our little guardsmen sounding the alarm! They devour the wagoneer soon as they see him for they know he carries news and gossip and goods. They have calculated and know that people can travel ten to twelve miles per day, and it takes about three days and nights for a shopping trip out of the cove. That's on average.

She heard John get up and his boots walk across the porch. He'd be returning to the fields, she knew. As for herself, she'd better finish this letter and get back to work too. Gardening, weeding, cooking, sewing ...ever so much needed to be done. But being busy suited her. And once she got it all done, she'd be able to escape into her very own enterprise of making her soap and butter.

Now, the other road, the Cooper Road Trail— remember it was built just a few years ago—was part of the Indian Trail, and now goes into Maryville. Maryville, to give you a sense of the geography, is more of a direct route for the western end of the cove. Admittedly, our little guardsmen don't watch that road as much; doesn't seem as well-traveled yet. But a man named Joe Cooper here wants to improve that road very soon—maybe in the coming years—and make it more of a wagon road. Hauling goods in and out of this place is difficult even in the best of weather. In rainy weather though, it's almost impossible. So we need better roads to be sure.

ᴄ↶Chapter Nine↷ᴐ

1850-1880—The Civil War Years

In 1850, the population was 685 in the cove and life was bustling. There were no more Indians, no more threats—or perceived threats. Some Indians remained in the area, but they stayed hidden in the dense forests and never showed themselves. They knew how to survive so well that the army never found them. Roads were better. Industry had touched their lives. Quilts covered every bed, food filled every kettle and pot, and children attended a sturdy school. Homes were caulked with clay, fires were always roaring. Strapping and muscular men tended the crops that kept them all healthy and happy. Wise and spirited women kept an eye on all. The eagle laid two more eggs, and sat on them with his mate, taking turns snatching fish from the creeks, and small rodents and rabbits from the fields.

But the people of Cades Cove were still largely cut off from the outside world, not in news so much anymore, but in societal issues and crises. Given their remoteness, only the most basic laws reached these parts. No one really told them how to live. No one told them what to do with their economy. They were largely self-governed; even when they *were* governed; it was mostly done through the church. And, there were no slaves in the cove. Not now, or ever. The families and their children and neighbors tended the fields themselves.

Perhaps a few hired hands were brought in here and there, but harvesting was largely a community-wide effort. They were extremely self-sufficient. No real government existed to tell them how to live. John Oliver, the Tiptons, Shields and Jobes were leaders, not governors. They kept order and were admired and respected; sought after for advice. But they did not govern any other man. Nonetheless, in America's first hundred years of life, its larger problems crept into this peaceful mountain valley in eastern Tennessee. At first it was just a slow-cooking rumbling of talk...and it occurred outside church one Sunday morning in 1859.

"John Brown went to Harper's Ferry!"

"Where's that?"

"Who's that?"

"Virginia. Some kind of abolitionist activator or somethin'. And he led those people in Kansas, some bloody Kansas thing a few years back."

"But they found him out! He was giving guns to the blacks."

"Oh boy..."

"They got him. Executed him."

Luraney and the rest of the women listened to the men and immediately began their own conversation.

"Well. These men have just started another war."

It wasn't quite yet war, but this event pushed a terribly divided nation much closer; so close that there was now no turning back. The nation was fractured—so much so that there were four different tickets for the 1860 Presidential election.

The news carrier boy called on his bugle upon his entrance into the cove on a cold November morning. Days had passed, but word had not yet reached the cove that Abraham Lincoln had won the election—thanks entirely to the Northern states. That event, coupled with Harper's Ferry, John Brown's execution, and other skirmishes, sent the Southern men into a deep anger. How dare they tell us how to run our own states! The South depended heavily on slave labor for their economy ...the North was going to abolish slavery! Their very way of life. Their source of money and security.

"Our interests are no longer safe under this Federal Government. They only care about what's happening up North. Well, that ain't right! We're part of the United States too!" The South was in an uproar. And so, many states withdrew from the Union. But not Tennessee.

Tennessee residents voted against secession, almost 65,000 residents voting against it. They wanted to work things out, settle down, thinking they were much better off as part of the bigger nation. Many states voted to leave the Union, some voted to stay. Some wanted to have a consistent message and law for the entire nation; some wanted to run their businesses according to the economic realities of their lives. States' rights! Slavery is wrong! Are all men created equal? Are we indivisible with liberty and justice for all? Every one of us?

Things did not settle down.

April 12, 1861 dawned bright in the cove. The springtime chores were well underway. Their animals readied for new life. Everyone went about their daily business. Everyone ...yet there were fewer of them now. Much fewer. For, the population as the 1860s came into existence dropped drastically to just around 300 souls. Though still prosperous, the nation's unrest had driven market prices down and grown children fled to seek their futures in the larger towns and cities.

As the sun shone on that spring morning in April, Fort Sumter in South Carolina was being attacked by South Carolinians. It was the south's militia, who just would not abide any more of the north's oppression of their way of life. A shell landed. Men scrambled. The eagle in Cades Cove flew back to its nest for the day. John Oliver stopped what he was doing and smelled something rotten in the air. *Decay*, he thought. *Something is decomposing.* He went further out into the fields to investigate and found nothing amiss. A beautiful spring day. No dead animals. No vultures circling. No commotion anywhere. All was well. Still, he was sure something was wrong. It bothered him all day, even though he found nothing at all out of the ordinary. That night he dreamt of the eagle, and, in his restless slumber, the eagle smashed into his cabin, as if he were blind, spewing blood everywhere. He never knew what happened to the eagle because he woke up with a start.

John rubbed his eyes and looked over at Luraney. Fast asleep. He smiled at her. The children were sleeping, the door tightly latched. Ol' Blue stood in the corner, nearby. The fire's underbelly of red embers remained hot. The dream did not melt away like they always did.

Rising from bed he walked out into the dawn's early light. Chilly. Clear. He sniffed. There was still a smoky rot in the air. But all was calm and peaceful. And, in the early morning light, the lone eagle flew overhead, slowly it seemed, flying from the south end of the cove towards the north. John felt his heart lift for a moment upon seeing America's symbol, freely roaming the empty air. He looked over the outside of his dwelling. No sign of an actual eagle smashing into his home. No blood. It was just a dream. All was well. What was wrong?

It would be days before he got the news.

The American Civil War had just begun.

At first, residents gathered in the middle of the cove, shocked that it had come to this. They were watching their smaller children, all in a group, walking down to the creek, tin pails in every hand. Sent to fetch water.

"We are fighting ourselves!"

"How did this happen?"

As always, they talked about how they relied on themselves, stood tall and strong; talked about how they were self-sufficient, and they'd get through it ...it don't really concern us does it? We're surrounded by mountains, we don't bother no one, *we are all neighborly. It won't affect us. Not too much.*

No matter how hard they prayed that the war wouldn't affect their idyllic slice of mountain life, most residents did take a side. They stood with the North, though they resided in Tennessee—the South's territory. These two worlds could not live in harmony. Some didn't quite understand the fuss. After all, the cove itself—the land—was not conducive to growing cotton; thus, they didn't need slave labor.

"We never had one slave here!"

"And I dare say, we never will."

"God's will is that we are all equal. Our Constitution even says it."

"But then there's that issue of taxation, and State's rights ...they just want to keep their way of life. Like we do here."

"The South wants *some* political control ...they're part of the country too."

"Indeed, slavery is wrong. But the North shouldn't be able to control everything. Don't the South have a say?" one of the Tipton boys asked.

"Yes, of course. But people aren't cattle. Or pigs. Imagine being sold! Imagine your children being sold! And never seeing them again!"

"A price tag on a human. Whoever heard of it?"

But humanity had indeed heard of it—plenty of times before. From ancient times and the earliest civilizations. Was slavery inherent in all human cultures? It appears so. The Hammarabi Code, that very early system of laws, recognized slavery. Egypt had them; their slaves even accompanied their owners to the afterlife. Greece. Rome. As early as the 18th-12th Century B.C.—the Shang Dynasty in China. Slavery is in the Bible. In the Torah. The Quran. Slaves were picked up via war, desperate times, growth, and kidnapping. Men, women and children were slaves. Blacks, whites, Jews, and almost every other race were slaves. In India, there are slaves recorded in the ancient language of Sanskrit. Rome's great civilization was dependent on slavery. How else were they to build the road, buildings, towns, aqueducts? Slaves served as priests and as janitors, in fields and in homes. In businesses and in palaces. Some slaves rose to become monarchs, sultans and even founded dynasties. They were the lucky ones. Russia, France. Italy. North Africa. North America. The Caribbean. Sugar, tobacco, cotton. How else could they gather all that was needed for human life and luxury? The Bronze Age had slavery. Ants enslave some of their own. On that note, don't humans enslave all sorts of breeds and races of animals?

It can be justified with the need for utility.

And an even greater need: Power.

Despite the neighboring North Carolina being "fully entrenched and quite healthy" in the use of slaves, East Tennessee was abolitionist, even "freeing, educating, and ordaining two black missionaries." And so, this one small geographical area of America was extremely divided. They may not have understood the full issues or consequences. They may not have grasped all the economics of the larger cities. Or the complete picture of state's rights. But these mountain folk were godly, moral people. Gentle and self-sufficient. Live and Let Live. They lived that way with the Indians for a long time. Until...well, they didn't like to think of their own John Oliver being part of the local militia that rounded up the last of the Indians, even the twelve Cherokee, who saved his very life that first winter of 1818-19. John pushed them on their long walk, away from these parts. The Trail of Tears. They never felt good about it, truth be told. But perhaps this was his, and the residents', chance to make amends. Their thinking was different now. They *hadn't* allowed the Indians their land. Perhaps some still thought they were perfectly right in their actions. But now, with the issues of rights and slavery, most of the cove's good men and women would choose the side of freedom.

And so it was that the majority of the cove residents, even if they didn't fully understand the totality of the issues or had conflicting views in the past, sided with the North. But a few backed the Confederacy, notably Daniel Foute.

Daniel Foute, always a leader in the community, the one with the can-do spirit, the technology whiz, the owner of the Cades Cove Bloomery Forge, owned numerous slaves, though not within the cove. His human property worked elsewhere in Blount County, Tennessee. For now, he remained a leader, but the whispering about his owning of slaves and "going Confederate" grew louder.

Soon, despite their best efforts to keep away from the larger problems of America, the War Between the States arrived directly at the doorsteps of the cabins and porches of the cove. It begged for men, food, and alliance.

"As of now, we've got twenty-one of our boys fighting for the Union, and twelve for the Rebs." Tipton reported one morning after Sunday church. They'd all met at Oliver's place since it was closest to the churches, and he had plenty of logs to sit on under the thick trees. The views were especially nice here on the northern side, and the ground was always dry. The men spoke for hours, but they were keenly aware that the women had all gone home with the children with barely a word.

The cove mothers' hearts were breaking until they became swollen sacs of sadness and worry. The odors and stains of war were not familiar to these hearty, peaceful women. And if they were, it had been a long time ago and hadn't involved their very own sons. They had enough to worry about! Nature, winter, cold, crops, childbirth, supplies ....The women knew exactly what to think. *Unlike that stubborn Foute!* they huffed to themselves. And they knew exactly whose side to be on. Sell children? Just because of their skin color? Their swollen sacs of sadness swelled even further with despair. Turning to God was the only thing to do at this time. Luraney's family Bible was on her lap every single night. Sometimes even in the afternoons on the chair on the porch. Or in the garden, in her hands, while she leaned up against a tree or the fence when it just got too much. It would be years before she was able to lay it down in peace, and sadly, not just because of this terrible war.

Though most of the women knew exactly their feelings, others were split, seeing both sides clearly; at times, their emotions wavering depending on what circumstances the seasons of the next four years brought. Wavering still when Rebels raided and seized food, livestock and other supplies from residents. A relationship with the war tugged at everyone—wavering between grudging tolerance and patriotism and opposition. Children had to become guards— blowing bugles to warn of invaders into the cove. Our own children! God's very innocents. Children as guards of war!

Women would've talked it out. Found some sort of compromise. Women talked and talked until they smoothed it over. Men fought. Damn these men to hell.

"It's Thomas' Legion!" they cried out from the mountaintops, the yellow-haired boy sounding his bugle as loud as he could. The children, boys and girls alike, recognized the different regiments now and were learning their movements. They could smell the rank bodies and horses moving up, through the ridges of the mountain peaks, way before they were seen. When the smell hit, and the children blew their bugles, the men of the cove grabbed their guns and showed their readiness. Typically, the human stink that threatened to invade, saw this activity and retreated. What were they to get? A cow or two? Some crops they'd have to tear out themselves? *There were an awful lot of guns pointed their way.* They moved on. *Perhaps to Chestnut Flats? That area of the cove to the southwest? Yes, that's where we'll try next. They aren't as well organized. Or, we can go around the cove and raid from the south...*

Danger surrounded the quiet cove. The eagle made a rare appearance, just for food and to quickly water by the creeks. It sensed the human tension emanating from the fields.

Most days were quiet. Life had to go on. Good and simple memories helped.

In the years leading up the war between the states, a transformative resident decided to settle in the mountain valley, who proved a valuable and cherished neighbor and friend. Dan Lawson had arrived back in 1856, on land he bought from his father-in-law, Peter Cable. Lawson proceeded to build his home near Cable's, which stood west of the stream. Dan was a quiet, humble man, very hardworking, with a moustache that seemed never to need grooming. He was always expanding his home, at first, a crude structure of rough-hewn logs like the rest of them, but in time, he used sawed lumber as he acquired properties, increasing his footprint and influence in the cove. "At one point, he owned a solid strip of land from the state line, on the ridge behind the house, crossing to the center of the Cove, to the top of the mountains in front."

The younger men of the cove, fascinated by his building skills, repeatedly visited to see and learn his ways. He was a modern day engineer and architect and relished in teaching.

"See here? The inside faces of the logs are to be hewn smooth with an ax. And the ceiling joists are to be dressed and beaded with a plane. Make it smooth! Chinks—battened inside with beveled poplar boards, and filled outside with brick and clay. The brick chimney now ...that's the heart of the home. Dig a hole in a nearby clay bank, and partially fill it with water. From the creek. The mixture needs to be worked to a proper consistency—pretty thick, you can use a hoe or paddle. Then, place into the molds to dry. I have some if you need. The bricks then must be stacked and fired. After cooling, they're ready to use." He paused as if contemplating, the professor in overalls. Then, he turned civil engineer…how to lay out the entire homestead?

"You can build small outbuildings for family pantries. We all have large families, eh? The one closest to the house can be the granary, and the other is a smokehouse. Granaries are fairly rare around here ...y'all know better than anyone, not much wheat is grown here. Some, to be sure. But corn ...corn is what we are—we're corn country."

Corn, a far more widely used crop, was stored in a corncrib, "which is another kind of building as you know. But you can make it better ...see here ...raise the ceilin' just a bit. Makes for better airflow." Dan Lawson continued. "Meat, of course, is smoked and salted, or you can smoke *or* salt—note the difference—and/or—either way, you know you got to preserve it. Then, store it in the smokehouse, which can be built right over here ...make it secure so animals don't go lookin' and tearin' up the place. Oh, look! An eagle." He paused to point his pupils towards a circling knot of feathers. Gliding from south to north, angling its body to turn, then from north to south, then back again. It seemed unsure of where to land; just kept flying.

"That is one big bird."

The war raged on.

One day, Confederate troops and recruiters showed up. Bugles didn't help them scamper to the next settlement, and they kept on walking into the cove. Dressed in rags, brown and gray semi-uniforms—if you can call them that—they headed towards a residence where a U.S. flag was flying. The knot of cove men immediately knew what they were out to do.

Firing a warning shot, the former bully of the cove, Jacob Tipton, yelled out, "Y'all better leave that flag alone. Or I'll shoot."

The Confederates stopped and squinted at Jacob, guns in hand. Then they looked at the approaching men, guns in hand all.

"Y'all aren't welcome here." Jacob cocked his gun again, raising it. His own sympathies mirrored most of the cove's. Practicality ruled, there were no slaves. No need for slave labor. They tended their own land. Freedom to live one's life was of the utmost importance. For everyone.

When the men didn't move, Jacob loudly proclaimed, in the most sinister tone he could muster. "Leave. Or we'll leave you dead. For the vultures to eat."

The Rebs consulted for a moment. As guns tend to do, it made them pause for a moment and think.

"Y'all better git outta here. Our vultures are big and hungry. There'll be no bodies to send home." Jacob's tone rose to deadly anger.

Tensions sprung to new heights just then. The eagle watched from as high a perch as possible as the rag-tag bunch of men stood for a long while, sometimes stepping forward a few feet in taunting actions. Guns drawn. Warning shots in the air. Guns pointed in both directions. Cove men stepping forward. Then, as they got closer, the Rebs jabbed each other's ribs and said some words to one another. Still, they stood in defiance. Another warning shot, this one closer. At that, the Rebs began walking backward, slowly, eyeing the familiar people that the eagle had come to know. This glaring, yelling, and peacock displaying went on for an hour.

The U.S. flag remained flying.

Jacob Tipton, the bully of the cove, was forevermore the hero of the *flagpole incident.*

Despite banding together, the cove residents were largely alone in the war and, despite prayers and large attempts to guard the area, the war and its events deeply affected the people. In 1863, the Confederate guerillas were ruthless. "Murder became commonplace," which terrified the residents. Some men went out hunting, or walking, or even tending the outer corners of their fields...and they would simply not return from the mountains.

John and Luraney's son, Elijah, had a son of his own by then, William Howell Oliver, born in 1857. The elder Olivers were so happy to be grandparents! Doting on the little boy, he was a bright beacon in this darkest of times.

Elijah, a thinker just like his mother, could not stop analyzing and dwelling on how the Civil War crossed through his family's lives, even seeing how it greatly affected his very own son. Sure, he was only six years old now, but to grow up amongst terror and daily and nightly watches and fear of murder was the most awful existence. And his own experience with being kidnapped ...being shot ... Why, what six year old had to see that? Deeply religious, he couldn't help questioning a God that would allow that to happen. What happened to picking corn with the fathers and uncles? Of swimming in the creeks without fear of who was behind the trees? Without fear of being picked off by a bullet from a screened mountaintop. Eating cornbread and stew outside on the porch on a warm summer evening? After soaking in a creek all day. What happened to all those ideal childhood memories they'd all had, and fondly remembered while standing under the trees, celebrating a wedding? It was all very heartbreaking not to simply work the fields and collapse after a productive day under a smiling sun.

The sun hadn't smiled in years.

Having picked up his mother, Luraney's, tendency to write letters to friends and kin, one late night Elijah felt a need to write down their wartime experiences. Why write such horrific happenings? Weren't they better left to be buried in the flames of the fireplace? Memories—even bad ones, *especially the bad ones, it can be argued*—are crucially important to all humans, and were teachable moments for little William and Elijah's other future children. History *is* life's instruction book. The manual so people wouldn't make the same mistakes. He laughed at that—*ha! Too bad people rarely read that manual...* His father loved Ben Franklin and he always remembered him telling Franklin's quote about the importance of documenting history: "Either write something worth reading or do something worth writing." And so, he documented his own small page of life's manual:

I did not enlist in the Civil War. Instead, my life was such: I would lay out and work in the fields of a day to make bread for my wife and children. I was a Union man in principle

Sometimes I'd go down in the settlement and get a yoke of cattle to haul feed and firewood; this was in time of the war between the states. On one occasion I went out after the cattle and the rebels caught me and kept me for two weeks. This was one of the hardest trials my wife ever went through. They shot me in the hand before I surrendered. But after this, I got away from them in the night and finally got back home. I can remember the shouts of my wife the night I come in.

On another time we were grinding our cane at the mill and boiling the juice kettles in a furnace. In this way the people would make their molasses—when all of a sudden two armed rebels came up, they stripped me off the horse and took me off with them, leaving our cane patch standing, and us nearly on starvation. We never got the horse back. When we seen them coming, I ran off and hid thinking they would take me, but when they started with the horse and scarcely got out of sight I came out and made for my gun. My wife caught around me telling me it would never do, that the whole army might come and kill us all, and so she constrained me to let them go, saying it would be better to lose the horse than it would be to lose some or all of our lives.

In the midst of this terrible war, the Primitive Baptist Church decided to cease worship services.

Decided?

It was forced! Russell Gregory, another early settler with eight children, cried. One of the solid families of the cove, the Gregory's were solid, upright members of their small society. This forcing—not deciding —of the church to close was true, for they were raided by the Rebels and the minister fled for his life. Thereafter, the people simply worshipped in their homes, under trees, in bed at night ...but they were outraged, which was just the thing that was needed for these religious people to spring into action.

Their religious and moral calling—to do good wherever you are, as stated in the Scriptures, and that God can call anyone to be a minister—extended from gentle hands coming together in the evenings by the hearth, to strong and sure hands guiding others under the shadows of an Underground Railroad deep into the night.

The cove had a secret railroad conductor: Dr. Calvin Post. Educated as a medical doctor, he was crippled as a youth, due to a boat boiler explosion while traveling on a riverboat. After a long recovery and mourning one of his brothers, who was killed in the accident, he finally made it to Cades Cove in 1847 ...almost two decades ago. His homestead was "a kind of botanical garden, a horticultural Eden." He called his home Laurel Springs. He had "beautiful native trees, walks and driveways bordered with trees, flowers in beds branching out from the house. There were acres in vegetable gardens, and other acres in fruit trees—apples, pears, raspberries, gooseberries, blackberries. There were crystal clear creeks which added charm and nature's own music."

But now, the kind and highly religious doctor worked to keep the residents on the side of the North "through his teachings and moral leadership," though most of them strongly bent to that side anyway. However, he wanted to take it a step further ...not only urging continued bending that way but taking moral and actionable measures. His whisperings to the other Union sympathizers were practical. *We are all to be careful not to have any evidence of this—no writings, no letters, no mass talk. But we are to be a grand station to help runaway slaves head north. The isolation is helping us—we have so many hiding places in the woods that even the dogs can't make their way up a mountain into a hiding hole or cave* they would nod their heads in agreement. If nothing else, they knew their land. *The biggest danger remains within our cove itself—some of these young, idealistic and gung ho kids side with the Rebels. They talk amongst themselves and are adamant with the ignorance of youth. They say that "the Yankees may outnumber us and they may kill all our soldiers, but never will get the Southern states." They are trying to hang onto their way of life. I guess we all did that, especially when we were younger. And didn't know better! They softly laughed, laughs of experience. I know I heard one of the boys proclaim, "State's rights, our rights ...nobody can tell us what to do!"*

"Well, you know that twenty-one young men of our cove joined the Union and only twelve joined the

Confederates ...but practically speaking, the majority are unable to join either side, given their lives and responsibilities here—we still have our farms to run! Either that, or we don't exactly know what they're up to—hiding out all day and night, or joining together in small bands to fight the Rebels?" Dan Lawson, Tipton, Shields, and the other men agreed. "We don't know some of what they're doing...we done lost track of some of those young boys. And their families ain't talkin."

John and Luraney, could not recall a time when there wasn't enough food, save for that first, starving winter. Now, with this fighting, even the Jobes, Tiptons, Shields, Lawson, and other families admitted that food was scarce. Crops were raided, so were animals and game. It's been years of this! We've had it!

Desperation and weariness seeped into the men, mostly the older men and they organized a resistance against the guerilla raids of the armies. And when the Primitive Baptist Church was raided, "forcing it to close and the minister to flee for his life," that sprung the congregation and actually the entire cove into even more action. They just had to organize a bit. They secretly pledged their help with the Underground Railroad. Nobody'd been caught yet. But how ever much they wanted to help, they knew they had to first save their minister and themselves, before they could save anyone else.

We have to save our community! Our way of life!

How dare they....

Anger.

"Them and us...we gonna mix." Jacob Tipton, the cove's bully hero, led the way.

We will "cut trees along the roads," and "conceal ourselves behind their blockades." *That should force those damn Reb guerillas to flee, leaving even our livestock behind...which they are after in the first place.*

What a boost in morale! Having a plan was both satisfying and comforting. And best of all, it worked. "See them Rebs run for their lives!" the young boys hollered, happy when they were able to ambush the Confederate soldiers, sending them running for the hills *faster than the creek rises.*

But when the Rebels realized they could no longer perform daylight raids, they resorted to coming at night.

Russell Gregory, with his eight children, and serious expression, had had enough of it.

He lived at the top of a mountain in the summer months with his wife, Elizabeth and his large family. This location was ideal to protect against the summer heat. Soon, it was even dubbed Gregory's Bald. But in the winter, he'd move his family down the mountain to its base, where it was buffeted from the bitterly cold wind and snow. A good, God-fearing, and humble man, Russell was a hard worker, was in a land partnership with Daniel Foute and two other men, and was very happy in the cove, loving mountain living. "Completely involved in all aspects of community life, he was a leader in the church and in the political, social, and educational life of Cades Cove. This sense of responsibility was complemented by an even temper and calm disposition. Frequently, he was called on to settle local disputes; his decision was seldom challenged or questioned."

That all changed during these trying times of war.

Gregory's son, Charles, was one of the few youths of Cades Cove whose sympathies lay with the Rebels. Youth is sometimes soiled with thoughts that differ from their parents, and not because they truly understand or agree with the other side, but simply because they have different ideas. Adolescents are quick to recognize the limits to their parents' power. Especially in mountain communities where kids grow up very quickly. They've seen animals birthed, understand how it happens, have seen death, attended church for the joy of a wedding and the tragedy of a funeral, and tended to pigs and cows and fields. They cry out, "I know what I'm doing!" when their parents try to meddle in their young lives. Secretly, most do respect their families, but talk behind their back, "their way of thinking is so old-fashioned. We live in a different world. *We* are at war." *They don't understand.* "We are at war." Forgetting that their parents also lived through war and hardships—even facing real starvation—they felt they were the first ones to ever live through conflict and deprivation and even moral confrontations.

Charles Gregory had joined Thomas' Legion from North Carolina. They're the ones that raided the cove, stealing livestock, even setting fire to farms, while the terrified residents hid in the mountains. Sometimes for days. His father, Russell, vowed to remain neutral, but that specific vow's deepest sincerity ran out after his son defected to the Rebel side.

Russell now vowed to take the Rebs down. Even if it made him a dead mess of a broken man having to fight his own son.

He and the rest of the now elderly, original men of the cove who settled this peaceful piece of Tennessee used their tried and true tree cuts blockade to stop an advancing group of Rebel soldiers. Piling the barrier high with limbs, they hid.

They waited patiently. Listened for every stick-breaking, every whistle riding the wind. Sniffed the air, waiting for the stench.

When the Rebs got very close, Russell Gregory's superior organization paid off. The first men in the line fired their guns, ambushing the surprised Confederate men. Two groups of cove men fought—one group fired, the other reloaded, then they switched. They knew exactly what they were doing, possessing everything from exit plans to resources to pure grit—a combination befitting any warrior.

"Aha!! They're retreating!" They whooped it up, feeling like the youngest of men again. "Git outta here!"

"Make it so the vultures eat your dead bodies!"

And indeed, the Rebs fled.

But they were not done. For Charles, Russell's son was part of that raid. And he was so enraged at the routing of his regiment at the hands of these backcountry kin—who were on the wrong side of this war, mind you!—that he plotted his revenge.

History is written by the victors. And it was so documented:

"Charles Gregory stepped forward and told the commanding officer of his group that he recognized the sound of the long rifle used by the bushwhackers as his father's rifle 'Long Tom'."

"There's Hell to pay now!" he had vowed.

"The Confederates snuck back across the Old Cherokee trails in the cover of darkness that same night. No horns would sound this time as they made their way down into the cove to affix revenge. Charles pointed out his father's house and the Confederates burst through the front door.

Russell Gregory gripped "Long Tom" and started to raise it to fire, but the Confederates were too close and Russell lost his balance and dropped "Long Tom." His hated enemy forced him outside and shot him dead with his own rifle and dropped it to the ground.

They delivered a message that they were in total control of Cades Cove."

"Murdered! As he rose from his bed!"

Horrified, Cades Cove, one and all, buried him in the Primitive Baptist Church's graveyard, with full military honors. As his family and neighbors gathered at the church to pay their respects and honor his sacrifice, they were able to see his gravestone, which read, "Murdered by North Carolina rebels." Outraged at the fact that his own son essentially killed him—he may as well have ...he had pointed out his father's home!—Russell Gregory's "reputation grew to legendary proportions among the cove people after his death," the victors documented.

Were they victors? Technically, factually, yes. But they'd lost a stable and solid member of their community in the most horrific of ways. They'd loved Russell Gregory. How could they ever get over that? Or what his very own son did to him? The glories and victories of war cease to matter upon such foggy silence. What could they do?

As always, they did the only thing they could do. Stick together. Tend to his widow and family. Keep the memory alive. Talk about him, ever-boosting his legendary status. And forevermore, the family made sure to keep "Long Tom" in the family. Something to hold on to, they said.

The eagle was seen more and more these days, his offspring soaring as well. The Civil War continued. As for the people of Cades Cove, things got better, but real and false alarms continued on a daily basis…letters written during those dark days relayed their existence as, "Living in terror of being killed and at dark we went to the bushes for our nights' rest." That terror made for sleepless nights, but also fiery, rebellious spirits, which stories were widely told.

One of the girls who was on duty with the horn was surprised by two Rebels one afternoon. Staring them down, when asked by the Rebels to give up her warning horn, she, "of the kind that used soft words" and who was raised a lady said, "Go to Hell!" And she ran off, the surprised soldiers chuckling at her moxie, and rode off.

They all chuckled at that tale …rooting for the young girl each and every time it was told.

As for Daniel Foute, why didn't he leave the cove and head further South where his loyalties lay?

"Why does he stay here knowing we are Unionists?

"I don't understand either. If my sympathies lay elsewhere, I'd certainly go to live among like-minded people. Feel weird stayin' where we don't think in common. 'Specially on somethin' so big."

Foute did not leave the cove; instead choosing to remain in the beautiful mountain bowl that kept up its magical tugging on his heart. The majestic pleated valley where creeks slide across its many faces and limestone rock worked over millennia to build up its body has a special pull for everyone who ever saw it. The Indians. Spaniards led by De Soto. The early settlers, beginning with John Oliver and his little family. The eagles.

No, Daniel Foute did not leave the cove, but sadly, Union troops, long knowing Foute's disloyalty to them, came in and arrested him, eventually putting him in jail.

"Sadly? Why say that?" Ruth Oliver exclaimed. "He was on the other side!"

"Yeah, but he was one of us. He's ours, no matter his strays." her sister quietly answered. To the Olivers, once a cove member, always a member. No matter if a bully or a traitor. Besides, God takes care of those people. Eventually, everyone had to answer. They had full faith in that.

He paroled, still under guard, and went to his daughter's home in Knoxville, Tennessee. His spirit and health in decline, but his heart intact, knowing he fought for what he believed in, Daniel Foute, the owner of the forge, the vast landowner and the embodiment of the can-do spirit of the mountain folk, soon died at his daughter's home.

1861 through 1865 saw America's great fight from within. It fractured the grand platter of the country almost to the point where no glue could put it all together again. But the American spirit picked up the pieces and slowly began finding the parts that fit together. You could always see the fracture points, and some chips remained, but it was still a complete and usable platter again.

Both the Union and the Rebel soldiers would return to those trenches, those stone fences they hid behind, those hilltops where they saw their brothers approaching, those cannons lying dead in the fields, and then, in the quiet, in the thick of the early morning mist, they would understand. So many battles. After the biggest and bloodiest battle in Gettysburg in 1863, it had rained all night long, soaking nine bodies of generals and another 8,000 or so souls left for God to dispose of. The creeks ran red, the bones of the dead exposed to God's eyes. Limbs were in heaps outside field hospitals, one woman—the wife of the town's largest cemetery, digging 100 graves herself while pregnant. Five thousand horses and mules lay dead. The next day, after the great battle between the north and the south in a beautiful field in Pennsylvania, where so many dead lay as payment for the costly battles of war, was the Fourth of July.

On April 9, 1865, peace was declared with General Lee's surrender at the Appomattox Court House in Virginia. But the cove would never be the same; truth be told, it hadn't been for years now. The eagle did not swoop so low and stayed in its nest for longer. Dry air felt a bit more stagnant and children were quieter when going about their chores. Life had a pall over it. Luraney's Bible stayed on her lap, while earth's icy face remained stoic. Clouds held their shape over the cove for days, leaden reminders of life's waning hours. Luraney's Bible had been the only comfort, for years now, and not just because of the war. Lately, she held on tight for days, only stopping for sleep and nourishment. If only to remember.

Because one day, two years ago, she knew. And she didn't let go for anything. For that was the day that John Oliver, the original settler of Cades Cove, her devoted and dearest friend and husband, father to Polly, Martha, Elizabeth, Lazarus, Elijah, Ruth, and William, no longer crossed his fields or the threshold of their porch.

*John continues to suffer; it's been a long time now. I worry ...yet hope ...*Luraney had written to his relations, continuing her letter writing habits. She had written these very words for weeks, months and today—later—she would write that she worried no more.

The Bible on her lap, sitting by his bed, her lovingly-made quilt covering his frail, old body, John Oliver crossed his heart one last time.

It was the fall of 1818, and I remember finally seeing the place I would die. I knew it immediately. It felt like home, though I never saw the place before. And I was happy to see it! It was five miles long and two miles wide. "Quite the burial place," Luraney had observed, not yet knowing that it would, in fact, come true. But I knew it would come true. I remember my eyes crinkling with a laugh. Quite perfect, I thought happily. That largest and broadest of chestnut trees. John's eyes slowly shut. No strength left. He knew he would never open them again. *The life I had here in Cades Cove was the great love of my life. I'm home.*

The eagle perched on a branch that sad day, February 15, 1863. All day the bird sat and watched the people, slowly moving a familiar human out of the house, tending to him, and then back inside, all their featherless wings wrapped around one another. Food being brought in on long platters, some showing chips and fractures, but still intact. The eagle would see the end of the Civil War, but John Oliver would not live to see his country mended. He died right in the middle of the action. Fitting it may have been; Oliver hated what the war was doing to his family and friends and to the community he founded, and though the North prevailed, the aftermath was devastating.

Still, John Oliver knew he had built something special. His family was close and his children were good citizens, good people, he had to admit. He and Luraney had done well. The best job possible. *Luraney—a very good wife she is. A wonderful, loving, strong mother to my children. She took care of me. I am lucky,* he often thought during his final days. The community was brawny, secure, close-knit. Despite shifts in viewpoints and issues in religion and war, he felt satisfied with what they built. *All because I took that chance long, long ago* ...And he *had* owned his own farm! A prosperous one at that. *My dream came true.* He sighed one last time, happy and ready on his deathbed that his lifetime of experience and the resulting wisdom and strength had passed on a better future to the next generation. *No regrets.* He was ready to meet his God.

It's okay. It was all quite perfect.

I'm home.

John Oliver made his final crossing.

Tears flowed, bleeding with the creek waters. Trees drooped just a bit more on that day, wilted in sorrow. The eagle did not feel like flying today; making one run for a fish, and that was all. A profound suffering ache settled over the cove; anguished air held its breath. The outstanding founders and leaders of their beautiful mountain cove were all gone: Daniel Foute, Russell Gregory, and, now, most profoundly, John Oliver, aged seventy.

Seventy years is a long time for folks living in the late 1800s. Seventy, Luraney thought.

Jesus' parables numbered at least 70 during his ministry. It's no wonder that John died at 70. Jesus' first five parables were in the Book of Matthew: salt of the earth light of the world, bird of the air are fed by God, consider the lilies and amazing flowers God has created, and they will be known by their fruits. These small phrases defined John Oliver. At his funeral earlier today, better words could not be found.

"John was a true light of the world for our community. He was the first."

"Salt of the earth—that's what John was. Such a good, honest, humble man. He was what a man should be."

"I'll remember him as one with his fields, his corn, animals, and most importantly, his family and his God. That eagle always soared over the cove, but did you ever notice...? It always was around John. Always. That bird of the air fed by God."

"The lilies, amazing flowers—all God made. But John, he made flowers and food too, and everything he touched turned to usefulness and life. He will be known by the fruits of his labors."

"We all loved him. The first."

"We are all here because of him."

The Cades Cove community said their goodbyes.

And now, Luraney, the widow of John Oliver, said goodbye, surrounded by her children, grandchildren, neighbors, relatives, and friends. Her lifelong companion, husband, father of her children, the one who took her to this God-forsaken land in the first place; only it was the most perfect place to spend her life. She didn't know it way back then, but now she knew it for certain. She asked God for strength. More than she'd ever asked in her life. Her John was gone, but she would see him again. Oh, she knew that. But it did not make today any easier. *He was seventy years old. All that he had accomplished...Family, farm, his own community!* She whispered to herself, *In Isaiah, it says that 'seventy years is the duration of days of a king."*

Dressed in black, Luraney let the tears flow. She knelt, with some effort, for she was sixty-eight years old herself. Her knees found the soft earth by the simple grave marker at the Primitive Baptist Church, in Cades Cove, Tennessee; surrounded by trees, they whispered their respects to a lifetime of memories honoring the king of Cades Cove.

After the bloody civil war in America, it was time for a new generation. April 1865 marked the end of the Civil War. General Lee, dressed in full dress attire, complete with sash and sword, surrendered his 28,000 troops at Appomattox. After all, he'd been Superintendent of West Point in 1852, and he intended to look the part, even now in defeat. Been called the "Marble Model" while a student at the military academy. General Ulysses Grant, a fellow graduate from West Point, accepted the surrender, still having immense respect for Lee. "Shushing a band that had begun to play in celebration, General Grant told his officers, 'The war is over. The Rebels are our countrymen again'."

All Confederate men would be pardoned. All were permitted to return home with their horses. Just in time for late spring planting. Nature waited for no one. Slaves freed. Reconstruction. Slow, but steady. A nation divided. How would they ever come together again? Were they ever together in the first place? Economic turmoil in the South. Everyone is adjusting to a new way of life. Slaves, white men, Indians forced West, Spaniards, Irish fleeing to America in the 1840s, their potatoes all rotting in the fields—all the inhabitants on earth were in a constant state of change. Nobody, no group, race or culture is immune. It is how we adapt to change that spells survival. And punctuates a degree of happiness.

Another year, 1866 began in Cades Cove, Tennessee. A new generation waiting in the wings. And, for another of the cove's princes, that was the last new year they would see.

Peter Cable would not live to the close of 1866. He had come with his wife, Catherine, so long ago, to this isolated bowl of fertile land and good hardworking people. Their children were raised here, he owned a lot of land. People from all around said of Peter Cable: "He could make most anything either of iron, steel or wood that was of use on the farm or in the shop or mill." His life was good, and he crossed through it like a straight, well-worn and reliable path—not too many rough parts—stopping often to meet lifelong friends and neighbors along the way. Now, he rested with the king of the cove, right near John Oliver, under a beautiful chestnut tree— the broadest and biggest—whose colors would turn yellow and orange in the fall.

Watching the old princes die and come to their final rest was what the chestnut tree seemed destined for. The light green leaves in summer had also seen Joshua Jobe die in 1863. The eagle kept the old tree company and watched as the stone was put into place: "In Memory of Joshua Jobe, Born September 15, 1785; Died May 3, 1863. He lived in Jesus & Died Looking Unto Him." He sired fourteen children in all.

Even further back, 1849 had seen the death of the large, red-haired William "Fightin' Billy" Tipton. He had also sired fourteen children, made his mark on his community, and left a sturdy home and livelihood for his family. He, too, died having lived in the bosom of his great love. And oh, was he a happy man for that! He died praying and preaching that his dear Cades Cove does something to a soul. It tells the truth, always, because it knows that if you are here, you can take it. No false protections. None of this special treatment, mind you. The Cove treated men as its equal, letting them think for themselves, experience life on their own terms. Not immune from the consequences though. No sir. The cove would take your life if you did not respect its wildness, its ability to snuff you out in an instant ice fall or with its roaring creek waters. Or if encountering one of its bears protecting four cubs. But if you did respect it, she was the most honest and loyal lover any man could hope for.

The eagle made a rare appearance now and then, but not with its same splendor. The old guard had passed away, paving the way for the new. What was this new guard like? As is always the case, the old complained about the young, but this time, with evidence to back them up. The young were "far less literate, deprived of the time and means of gaining an education, and were provincial and introspective to a degree that would have surprised and saddened their predecessors." Luraney still wrote to hers and John's relatives back home— what was left of them *Everyone was getting old. And passing away,* she sighed, sealing her envelope and waiting for the bugle to sound, announcing the mail boy. *Nothing was the same.*

People of the cove were more isolated than ever. War had killed some of them off, made them wary, and even angry at outsiders. They tried to need nothing, or very little, of outsiders. But they did have some new ways of injecting some fun and diversion into their nestled little circle. Why, they even began distilling their own moonshine, but *don't let any of those Olivers find out. They are opposed to it to the ends of the earth,* the younger folk carefully whispered.

Chestnut Flats, on the other hand, was the place just on the outskirts of the cove proper to obtain that moonshine, and it was good too. Yeast, corn meal, sugar, and water. *So clear coming outta that sill, that you just bottle it up, and wash the worries away.* But not on Sundays.

The offspring of the Olivers, Tiptons, Jobes, and other early settlers intermarried, combining and creating new topics of gossip, and introducing new culture to the cove. They discussed most everything together, went to church, visited, kept their parents' farms tended and even expanded to newer, better methods and construction. But the Oliver children were never part of the moonshine talk.

If it was good enough for the American Revolutionaries—you know, they didn't pay a lick of taxes on the drink if they made it themselves—it's good enough for us!

Oh, that Whiskey Rebellion. Yeah, I heard of that.

We all heard of it! We hear the same things at the same homes and churches! Our kids hear the same things at the same schools. We live the same lives.

The Olivers don't. They're good livin' folk. Perhaps a bit too strict. But they're salt o' the earth people. And they were here first. Revered since our beginnings. Gotta respect 'em.

One and all agreed, silent for a moment, understanding the deep roots of the Oliver family.

Yeah, well, I've heard talk of some kind of Prohibition.

Laughter. *That will never happen!* But then, they had thought that about the Civil War too.

The laughter died down. *At least, it hasn't happened yet.*

By 1880, only 449 people remained in the cove; still a good amount, but of these 449 men, women, and children, still mostly of the same original families, only 45 surnames were recorded as living here as the new decade dawned. Proving that the war continued to cast a palled shadow over their lives, the fact that the population did not rise showed the tighter-knit, keeping to ourselves, saddened spirit that blew through the fields.

The economic depression after the Civil War was devastating for the Southern states. Their whole way of life and infrastructure of their economics was literally destroyed. Slavery was outlawed after the war, of course, which paved the way to sharecropping and tenant farming. Now, slaves who were once owned by other men entered into contracts to work the land in exchange for a portion of the crops. But neither landowner nor laborer made any money; in fact, most landowners were made *worse* and owing even more money, even after the crops came in. Cotton was too cheap. What could be done? The residents pondered over and over, all the while having a sneaking suspicion that the "Golden Age" of Tennessee agriculture lay way back in the 1840s and 1850s. A lifetime ago.

The aftermath of the war saw numerous pathways to possibly return to that Golden Age, but the new generation of cove inhabitants collectively thought, *since we are isolated, our solutions must come from within. Oh, we can follow what the rest of the country is doing, but we have to do what's good for us. No one's going to help us out here.* And so, the people "made every effort to distribute all the necessary components of life to needy friends and relatives" in our decimated south. But beyond that, the cove's souls tried to get on with business as usual. They worked their fields with their own families. They were self-sufficient, yet jumped to help one another whenever needed. Social life still revolved around religion and harvests.

We have a sense of community here in Cades Cove that no one else has. And with no more Rebel raids, we can finally try to settle in as we did back in the 40s and 50s. With a few tweaks of our own, perhaps we can recreate what our parents had. Back when the outside world did not interfere. Back when life was good....

⚶Chapter Ten⚶

1880-1890—THE MILL

Not everything stood stock still and devastated during the war and post-war years. In fact, their very isolation had actually helped the cove families move forward in some very profound ways. Progress had occurred, and the cove saw a boom to their community when the Mill was built.

Five years after John's death, and three years after the war between the states ended, the John Cable Mill was built. 1868 saw this watershed moment in the cove and it changed life forever. Now that they'd had it for over a decade, the southwest corner of the cove was the hub of life within the mountain community. Nestled in the woods, right off the road, the mill's exterior was tall, with a wooden walkway leading into the interior. Stopping right before entry, customers would look to the left and see that big wheel in continuous motion from the chute of creek water, keeping it going and going. It was covered in snow in winter, gold and amber leaves in fall, dogwoods in summer, and the greenest of maple leaves in summer. Inside the mill, the large grinding stone strained and groaned out whatever the cove needed to keep going. Through the devastating raids of war and the crawling stages of Reconstruction, it kept turning. Eagles circled, looking to pick up the small rodents that scurried under the buildings. Little creatures are always looking for scraps. The wheel kept going.

John P. Cable was the nephew of Peter Cable, who, he recalled fondly, was one of the founding residents of the cove *When did Uncle Peter settle here?* He had to think of the exact year -*that's right, it was back in 1825.* When he recalled this date, he was solidly situated in 1867, the year before starting his mill.

Forty-odd years later it was since Uncle passed through here for the first time. Hard to believe all that time had passed. And Uncle Peter had settled here with his wife, Aunt Catherine. Uncle always spoke of towering trees, pine, oaks ...abundant game, Indians, fertile soil. The best neighbors a man could ask for. He remembered such talk in over half his memories. And now he was here. *The current member of the Cable family. One who is overdue for a change and yearning to add to the mountain community that Uncle so raved about and loved.*

Though not born in the cove itself, John Cable was proud that he hailed from one of these few, cherished founding families of the cove. It gave him instant credibility amongst the inhabitants. *Heck, we heard about you from when you were toddling,* he heard from more than one person when moving into the cove. Which was true—not much in life was secret. And not much had to be. Everyone knew everyone else's family around these parts. They knew each other's characters. Who is the black sheep? Who is extra-reliable? Who can shoot his gun best? Fastest? With the best aim? Whose girls would make good wives? And can cook? Embroider as if trained in Europe? Whose family was trustworthy? Who to stay away from. It was all very comforting, most everyone would agree, because no one could hide their true nature, either in person or in reputation. Yes, most would agree. Most of the time.

A year after his 1867 arrival, the mill was born. Corn was still king. So central to life for both humans and livestock. A Native American plant—*Luraney Oliver often thought of this irony* —corn was the most important crop, and thankfully, the most abundant. It grew with minimal attention, not like the high-maintenance crops of cauliflower and that water-sucking celery.

The men and women of this gorgeous mountain fertile bowl often talked corn and what to do with it.

Corn on the cob, of course.

Cornmeal, to make biscuits, bread.

Fried corn.

Grits.

Popcorn. When it's in that big pot over the fire, it sounds like firecrackers goin' off right in the house. Mama leaves for the porch until it's all done. Says it gives her a God-awful headache.

Creamed corn.

My mama makes corn brooms every two months. Always sweepin' the dirt off the floors!

We use the shucks in our mattresses and our chair bottoms. It's a great filler.

Grains, stalks, foliage feed our animals.

I hear they're tryin' to make some kind of corn oil. But they ain't done it yet.

Mush. Hominy.

Fermenting into alcohol.

Don't tell the Olivers. Don't tell our mothers.

That produced a chuckle amongst the men.

The women pretended they didn't like it, but at the end of a hard day, some of them partook in small doses as they read their Bibles. Because the Bible even says that alcohol is fine in moderation. It's the excess that does you in.

First though, for many of these products, corn had to be ground into meal. "Millers were farmers and John Cable was no exception." John grew corn himself, and he knew how to handle it. An organized man, he devised a system where he could juggle both crops and mill, and on the first Sunday before he opened the community mill, he gathered everyone he could, who were walking from their respective churches, in front of the tall building. The water wheel was already churning with water from Forge Creek, just upstream. The mill was just about complete.

One and all were in awe that such a high-tech and important service was actually right here in Cades Cove!

"Oh, we know the Greeks and Romans had them. All the great empires used the wheels, water; ground their flour and corn. They needed bread after all." John Cable proudly stated to the crowd a little bit of the history of what he'd built. "We wanted to bring that same service to our little empire. Right here."

Grateful heads nodded. Indeed, their little mountain empire was flourishing.

He took them on a tour of the grounds and then set to educate his friends and customers on his system.

"Here's a bell." He began.

"Wow, that's a huge bell." One of the children stated, looking at the metal bell mounted on top of a pole right beside the building.

"When you need the mill, ring the bell to call me from the fields, or orchard—wherever I happen to be."

"That bell can be heard all the way to Knoxville!"

John laughed. "Exactly! I will always hear it. I'll run in from the fields and grind your corn. And then, a nice cornbread can be on the dinner table every evening."

And indeed, there were no more tub mills or crude ways to grind right on the homestead property, no more going to nearby Tuckaleechee Cove for grinding. It was all right here in this tiny empire embraced in a powerful mountain bowl.

"It's more than a mill now. Have you noticed? It's only been a few months and already, it's where the entire community gathers. Not the churches, though they're certainly our traditional meetin' places. They're still hubs of course. But we've evolved. The mill is now where we have our congress."

"Your father sure has transformed Cades Cove."

Becky was proud of her father. She ran, carefree, to the creek to splash in the rays of the smiling sun *No better place to be a kid. Can you imagine me in a town?* She laughed to herself at that thought. *Bonnets and shoes and sitting at tea tables? No way. Not I! The fields and creeks is where I belong.* Unbeknownst to her today, the fun and freedoms of a cove childhood were actually preparing her for the many skills that would be necessary for the immense trials of her future. But that's for far down the road. Today, there was a smiling sun and a little Oliver boy chasing her through the trees. No matter. *He'll never find me! I know all the secret spots.* And she crouched in a cave high up on a mountaintop, watching an eagle fly free for the rest of the day. When twilight came and the sun tucked itself in for the night, she walked home. Leisurely, through bear hotspots, coyote howls, and unknown spirits of the mountains. She was never scared. And none of her playmates—boy or girl—could ever find her.

Luraney Oliver, during all these years, remained a steadfast matriarch of their society. Boasting around 448 souls now, the fields remained bustling with activity. Her grown children and now, grandchildren surrounded her like a warm wind. *There really are broad, universal themes in human lives aren't there? Events and feelings that touch us all. That repeat themselves. Children have traits of their fathers, mothers, grandmothers ...I see resilience and work ethics in all the young Oliver souls. Elijah is just like his father. Elizabeth shows a lot of myself. The others are mixes of all of us ...a perfect merging of truth and warmth. And the grandchildren! So much of our ethics lie safe in their small hearts.*

She was proud, her heart filled with pride. She sat on the porch, in the cane-backed chair and scanned the cove. Her family was busy with their everyday lives. There they are out in the fields. Over there, weeding the kitchen garden. Two boys were by the barn, leading stubborn horses out to the creekside so they could clean the stalls. Buckets to be filled. Cows to be milked. Corn to be ground. Bread rising.

The experiences of watching many lives is one of the keys to wisdom, she thought to herself as her hair blew in the breeze. Her quilt was on her lap, but she wasn't sewing. Her eyes no longer allowed it. Instead, the quilt's only purpose now was to protect her knees from getting a chill, and to steady the pot of fresh green beans she plucked at.

One can only live one life, she caught herself at that thought, her eyes betraying an entry into deep thought, as the beans sat in her hands. *Just one? What about doing different things? Changing as a person? By taking risks, gathering experiences, you really may live out numerous lives. She knew it to be true. How amazing is that?* She thought, plucking at a bean. Then, an inner battle resumed, and her thoughts roamed from one hand to the other.

In the end though, you only are *just one person. One that God made. Even if you change, you still have just one childhood; your memories. Yours alone. Only you know what you really thought of the marriage bed. Only you know the deep gashes of suffering and hardships. The ones that never quite fully heal. And you are glad of it, for they are reminders. Your children being born—the pain and the crying relief—the only time in your life that you prayed for your child to cry. Private thoughts. Ones that you don't even want to have. All contained in one vessel. There certainly are universal human themes and experiences. All largely the same. The difference is, we view life through different lenses. We may all pick apples but our perspectives and experiences will be different. Some will remember the smell. Some, the touch. Some the tediousness of the chore of picking them or baking them. Some, the taste. Or the sight of red orbs of freshness. Watching others and learning how they view apples ...now that is the key to living other lives. Traveling to other worlds.*

Luraney, the thinker, even more so now in her old age. John had been gone for nearly ten years now. Could it be a decade already? She smiled and remembered their seasons and times. *That first winter...* She shuddered at the still-vivid memories of starving and the fear of Indians. *The ones who saved us with their dried pumpkin.* John revered those pumpkins. Different lenses. Jobe spoke of this new place with free land with such enthusiasm, way back in 1818. When she got here, it was all she could do not to turn and never look back. Free land? They'd nearly had to pay for it with their lives! The battle had raged within during those dark, winter days. Terrible sleepless nights, so many in a row. But two cows had brought peace. *Two milk cows. And pumpkins.* Luraney laughed at her memories, the best and the worst of them. She had observed them all. How many lives *have* I lived? It was hard to count. Luraney laughed at her memories, the best and the worst of them. She had observed them all.

Jolted just then by a distraction. A welcome one. For one of those cherished results of this wise woman came running up to her to interrupt her thoughts, yelling "Granny! It's sorghum time!" She always welcomed such interruptions: baby faces, soft hair flying and springy bare feet that she always sought the sight of through her lens. So many lives. Miracles, all.

"Granny, it looks like an orange flowering corn!"

Sorghum molasses—that sweet, nutty savory so popular in the mountain diet. As usual, sorghum molasses time was a social event. Just like berry picking, corn shucking, and snapping beans between practiced fingers. The sorghum cane stalks were cut in the fall, and stripped of their leaves. The children played swords with those stalks, and they were allowed to, for then they would run through the rollers of the mill, powered by a strong horse or mule, pulling a long pole in a circle. Their running turned into the inevitable pushing of the poles, thereby assisting the animals.

"How long does it take, Granny?"

"Well, see here. It's all crushed right? And we got a lot of juice. Now, we boil for, oh, four or five hours until it's nothin' but syrup." Luraney loved showing her grandchildren, having already passed on this process, as well as her soap and butter recipes, to her grown children. To her delight, her soap and butter were still extremely sought-after items.

"It's nice and thick, see?" She spooned up a lovely thick liquid from the large kettle.

"Oh, yes. Pancakes like that!" the boy exclaimed, Luraney tousling his hair.

"Indeed, they do. They soak it right in."

"But I know the Jobes and Tiptons use honey and maple syrup too. Sometimes maple sugar."

"Indeed, they do. I prefer sorghum, but I love honey too. Put it in some of my soaps. Makes it very ...lathery." Luraney patiently explained.

"Why don't we just use honey all the time?"

"Yeah," the other child piped in. "There's bees everywhere."

It was true, as she looked at the children's tamed and natural playground. Red maples, dogwoods, sourwoods, pines and oaks. Sourwoods were blooming now in July providing nectar for their prized sourwood honey.

Luraney sat down while the children looked her straight in the eye. Her wisdom was legendary and they knew she had a good answer for everything.

She smiled and gathered them in her arms, so many of them!

"Why use sorghum and not honey." She said it like a statement. "Listen closely….bzzzzzz!!! She made a buzzing sound and her gentle fingers poked at their little bodies and bellies, causing them to laugh hysterically. *Oh, what a sweet sound.*

"Because you see? It's safer."

Little Becky Cable was a grown woman as the cove turned towards 1887. Just over a hundred years into the beginnings of the great experiment that was the United States of America, but only twenty or so removed from the massive rift that almost broke the entire undertaking. Some likened it to the ultimate sibling rivalry war. But the two siblings were mending fences, and its parent—loved or loathed depending on the lens—was reburied with his wife in Springfield, Illinois that April. The parent's tombstone read: Born February 12, 1809. Died April 15, 1865. Twenty-two years ago. The name on the new stone where the parent was re-lain was still fresh: Abraham Lincoln. 1887. In May, a gas lamp caught fire at a Paris Opera, killing 200 people. The cove residents prayed for their souls, having read about it in the papers. June saw the Golden Jubilee of Queen Victoria over in England. And another gas lamp in Exeter caught fire killing another 200. They prayed for another 200 souls.

"Some gentleman named Otis patented an elevator. It can take one, in a car, up as many stories as can be built!"

The world was whizzing by from an ever-growing population who boarded trains, stayed in comfortable hotels, and built businesses all over the globe. People were better fed than ever. Thomas Edison was working on something new he called a light bulb with electrical currents passing through metal wire, somehow heating it until it glowed.

Becky and her brother, Dan Cable, were among the Cades Cove residents who read about all these happenings of the outside world. They were thankful to know of them, but equally grateful to live within their sphere where life went on as usual. Nature is ruthlessly efficient, without need for sudden innovations. Or the next best new and tasty thing. Trees, good soil, and healthy animals were all sharing skies that had clawed the tops of mountain peaks for millennia, exposed to both the warm winds and dark injuries of man.

Becky and her brother, Dan Cable were operating a successful general store and later, ran a boarding house. Up until 1873, most everything was bought at George Snider's store which was near the cove, but not within its boundaries. One could buy most anything: clothes, shoes, hats, seed, cloth, tools, machinery. Mr. Snider was good to the cove residents, extending credit and giving generous discounts. Becky and her brother did the same. Competition was minimal; there were plenty of customers to go around, and though most grew or produced what they needed as far as food, the large families always seemed to need cloth for clothes, shoes, and sacks and sacks of coffee and sugar and tea. Neighboring Chestnut Flats had experienced a boom in population after the Civil War, and boasted a mill or two, a distillery, and two schools. They too, visited the store as they meandered around the area. Reconstruction in America was ongoing; the scars healing. Things were better and better.

With a population of nearly 500 in the cove, and nearby communities of hundreds of people, other services prospered as well. There were woodworking shops and blacksmiths—both very important to a pioneer life. In her letters, Luraney was not shy about describing these particular craftsmen: "They all have strong, large muscles, a must for those heavy saws and hammers. The muscles gleam with sweat; a hard life for these men. Their wives are constantly filling the stew pots to sustain them."

Blacksmith shops held a dazzling array of axes, drawknives, adzes, bolts and bits, chains, hooks, bull tongue plow, and wagon tires, all key components of farm life. Iron from the fire is very malleable and capable of being reshaped from one tool to another. Repaired bits and pieces that cut, dug, hung, bore through and held together everything were scattered around the low-ceilinged wooden building, with wide slats for plenty of ventilation.

Such heat emanates from these most important of places! It was amazing that nothing inside, or even the building itself, ever caught fire. But they knew what they were doing; the forge and bellows being right in the middle, forcing concentrated air under a fire fed from coal or charcoal. This was what made it very, very hot—enough to work the iron.

"Usually, it's gotta be around three thousand degrees for us to work the iron." The blacksmith would explain to his customers. "How d'ya stand it?"

"It could get stuffy and smoky inside, but the wide slats made for surprisingly good ventilation," he'd say. "But be sure to stay behind the door." The half-door—the upper part open, the lower one shut, was always present for safety, especially for the little ones. The cove children hung around often, watching the always welcome sight of smoldering wisps of fire. It meant repair, putting things back together, making doors tighter, and getting their family back to work. It was fascinating to watch the rugged hardness of iron be manipulated into graceful curves and useful devices.

"Why, we use our blacksmiths more than our doctors!" they would observe.

It was true. Mothers and daughters knew all about abundant healing herbs—witch hazel for all kinds of broken skin, St. John's Wort for sedatives and pink turtlehead for indigestion—and they could heal most ailments without need for a doctor. But blacksmiths ...well, not everyone could trim the nails of a horse and set shoes on the beasts. Kicking, squirmy, and moody horses were dangerous; blacksmiths had to have that special soothing way or the job would never get done. Kitchen knives may have been much coveted but nothing was more sought after than horseshoes. Horse and wagon being the only mode of true transportation, they were the ones who could keep these living machines of the farm going. And get the family farm back to its full function.

Woodworking shops were much needed as well. Lumber milled on site was used for, well, everything. Homes, barns, even in the repair of churches. In the harsh elements and especially during icy winters and wet summers, wood rotted and had to be replaced constantly. Using water power, ramps helped logs along to the floor of the mill where, "after the first cut, the log has a flat side, then is rolled 90 degrees on the carriage to put the flat side down. Then, a second cut, like the first, is made, starting to square the log." But besides logs for buildings, woodworkers crafted countless chairs, chests, stools, tables and beds. There were even special carvings that could be made for decorative and special pieces of furniture.

Blacksmithing and woodworking—special skill sets that, once arrived at the cove, were highly prized, cultivated, and cherished. Such resources and materials were a must for an isolated, yet savvy and self-sufficient mountain community.

The hustle-bustle of everyday life had residents busy from morning until night. The rhythms of nature danced their way through both beast and human, its beauty giving pause, an escape from the toils of farm living.

But of course, one cannot escape death, which never stops; a thread that weaves its way from a mother's arms to the cold mound where salvation begins.

Coffin makers and stonemasons for grave markers were constant professions, guaranteed to profit even in the toughest of times. Different types of stone were used depending on the burial. Infant burials could be a simple rock, no name, no dates. There was often no time. Being Baptists, and based on their reading of the New Testament, there was no baptism of infants. They couldn't believe in anything yet— too young—and only believing adults could be baptized. But there had to be some comfort, some sort of reasoning. Humans cannot fathom a baby dying for no reason at all. And so, they would bury the babies, always in white, and read from Genesis: "Since we are to judge of the will of God from his Word, which testifies that the children of believers are holy, but in virtue of the covenant of grace, in which they together with the parents are comprehended, godly parents ought not to doubt the election and salvation of their children whom it pleases God to call out of this life in their infancy."

The churches each had a cemetery on the grounds. And every single Sunday—at least, if not more often—Luraney and the others would join in the procession of residents who lost loved ones. No family was immune; in that, everyone was equal. They would walk, hands behind their backs, smiling with solemn memories and filled with wishful hope and faith to see them again. The silent stones sat there, staring back, most with warmth; some with regret and unsaid words. Luraney knelt on the quilt she'd brought with her to cushion her grief, though it was difficult for her now. Her knees creaked and groaned, screaming in protest. Still, she knelt every Sunday and most Wednesday afternoons.

"John," she whispered, touching the gravestone with wrinkled, crooked fingers. "I know you hear me." She glanced around. Her friends and neighbors were on their own knees, in their own worlds. "I think I will see you soon. I feel...tired."

Luraney felt the breeze just then. "John?" She looked around. Deep in prayer, she felt his presence and somehow, she knew she would be in his arms once again. For eternity. She did not wish to leave this world, her children, grandchildren....but when God said her time was...

"John!" She opened her eyes at the brush against her cheek, just in time to see the eagle on a low branch, staring straight at her.

Bud Gregory, of the Gregory family who arrived in the cove early on—the ones who were in constant remembrance of Russell Gregory, and who had kept his rifle, "Long Tom," in the family—made coffins free of charge for the community. Elijah, the second son of the Olivers, had warned him days earlier.

"Put in an extra layer of white, and shape the coffin to fit—it can be thinner than that." He pointed to the walnut box. "Thank you, Bud." He bowed his head. "I will let you know when to bring it."

"Tell your mother my best wishes."

"I will." Elijah stepped outside of the woodworking shop and began walking east towards the Oliver homestead, where he resided with his own growing family. There was that eagle again, the one that always seemed to fly around their particular slot of land.

Oh, there was a time where I needed to fly just like that eagle. I went to other places. Had to. I wanted to see life outside these fields hemmed in by mountains on all sides. But the war came. My family seemed so far away. The war stopped, thankfully, and I needed to come back to my birthplace. These trees, the deer by the creeks, otters frolicking, bear, our dogs. My memories. The eagles. The Oliver homestead. Sometimes, I can't fathom how it all happened. I am now the proud owner of the land that my father risked so much to gain. How about that?

The eagle landed and perched high in the tree right outside the Oliver homestead. It did not ruffle its feathers. It stood motionless, bowing its head to watch the human activities below. Elijah was there in another few moments, knowing his sisters and aunts were inside, while the rest of the family watched his face as he suddenly ran up the path from the golden fields. His eyes met theirs and not a word was spoken. Everyone knew within minutes.

"The Matriarch has passed."

All that previous night of Saturday, November 24, 1888, Luraney Oliver was never left alone. She was 93 years old. Memories hovered over her body, unwilling to let go. In the morning, the procession sang "Hark from the Tomb," and filled the pews of the Primitive Baptist Church with every single person who resided in the cove. It didn't matter what religion they were—Primitive, Missionary, Methodist; no split churches were even thought of today. They were all one on this sunny late fall Sunday, to honor the Daughter, Wife, Mother, and Grandmother of Cades Cove. Lucretia Frazier Oliver would be sorely missed. *Salt of the earth. One of God's best.*

Buried with her husband, the gravestone read "First Permanent White Settlers of Cades Cove."

After the burial, the mound was towered with flowers.

"Elijah, I am so very sorry for the loss of your mother." The man put a hand on the young Oliver's shoulder. "Look at all those flowers. I've never seen such a sight."

Elijah thanked the man, a good friend of the family while holding back tears. They were all God-fearing and all believers to the core. But even through the clarity of salvation and Heaven, death on earth has a way of opening up a hole, of shifting one's life permanently. Every mother's child becomes a victim of loss.

"You know, let's get out of the Scriptures and Bible for a moment. That Florentine Renaissance man's thoughts on death will comfort you, I hope, at a time like this. What was it he said?" His younger brother Bill, known to be a scholar of classics, was talking, "Oh yes, he said 'As a well-spent day brings a happy sleep so a well-employed life brings a happy death'. He must've said that after he painted the Mona Lisa."

"Speaking of that, Elijah ..." Noah "Bud" Ogle, another dear neighbor said just then. "Your mother died the death that corresponded to her character—peaceful, honorable, and surrounded by love."

"That's beautiful, Bud. Thank you, much. I will remember that." Bud had 400 acres in the cove and some of his family lived over in White Oak Flats. "But most folk these days are referring to it as Gatlinburg," he answered when Elijah asked about how the extended Ogle family was faring.

"Ah, I'll have to remember that next time I'm 'round those parts."

Tributes and honors poured forth all day from the sad mouths of the Cades Cove residents. They had never known a cove without Luraney Oliver. And they were still not used to a cove without John Oliver. Now, they were both gone.

Later that day, when friends would typically escort the family back home, Elijah lingered under the trees, staring at the gravestones of his parents. *The front porch where quilts hung to air and dry. The wooden fence harnessing the smells from the garden. The harness smells of horses, along with the earthy aromas of cattle and pigs. Corn growing and cornmeal biscuits sizzling in the skillet. What a life mom and dad made here! Mom's butter and soap—so rich and the best within a hundred miles! Perhaps the best anywhere. What was it that mom said back then ...she said she almost hated this place. Regretted ever coming here. But then, she settled in. Adapted was the word she used. Bloom where God planted me. And just last week, Mom told me specifically, "My son, I could never have imagined another life. The Cove is the place I was supposed to be. Your father was right. And I am grateful."*

Elijah wiped away tears with the back of his hand. He was alone now in the cemetery, the day light's waning hours. The mother of Cades Cove—his mother—rested under the largest and broadest chestnut tree beside her beloved John. For eternity.

They were the very first ones.

He slowly rose and turned to walk home. The eagle was still present, standing as still as before, peering with dignified eyes at the young man rising from the great pile of flowers on a fresh mound of dirt.

Rebecca "Becky" Cable would never get over what her father had done to her. As a girl, she has always liked playing leapfrog in the creeks with Steven. They spent so many hours climbing trees, following each other while doing chores, and tracking that one small black bear they always found on the northern slopes. Steven could finish her sentences; they had always gotten along. Even in silence, sitting high up in a tree pretending they were eagles, they liked each other's company above all others. A childhood playmate became a crush, and then, a love.

And then, her father had done something. Or said something.

She never got a completely straight answer, but he did admit he interfered. He admitted it! *He is not the man I want for you. Why not, Father? I know him! He's from the cove. What more can I seek? You need an Oliver. Or a Tipton. A Jobe. One of the founders. A Lawson. An Ogle boy. Even an outsider would be preferable. Steven's family ...well...I spoke to Steven and even he agrees with me. He won't bother you again. He doesn't bother me, Father! Well, he won't anymore. I refuse to marry anyone else. I won't do it! Do not speak to your father in such a way! I won't marry anyone then!* Her father had stopped her from marrying her love. The one person who allowed her to be herself. High spirits and sharp tongue and all. Becky never forgave her father.

Not quite going to the extreme dramatic route of Romeo and Juliet, nonetheless, the star-crossed lovers would never meet again. The poisoned sword of young heartbreak always leaves a deep scar; *it certainly feels like a death.* Steven's family moved away from the area shortly thereafter, without a word of goodbye. *Did Father know he wanted to say goodbye and stopped him? Do I know – truly - that he would've never left without saying goodbye? Was Steven trying to save me this heartless heartache?* Thoughts of being protected sometimes crept inside. *But surely, Steven would've stayed. He wanted to marry me. He said so our entire lives! Oh, I will never forgive*

Father. If he thinks I will marry anyone else, he is mistaken. Steven will always be my one and only love. I will never marry!

By the spring of 1896, Becky was still true to her word, never marrying, and known as a spinster, an independent, unmarried woman. Long gone, sadly, were the days where Becky was proud of her father's mill, the hub of the community. Much anger had replaced that feeling. Gone also were the days to splash carefree in the creek, in the middle of the rays of the smiling sun. Rebellious and spunky by nature, she was now affectionately referred to by everyone as Aunt Becky.

Boys and girls grew up in their traditional roles, which worked very well for most every civilization. This tradition was kept in the cove and was a large part of their success. Traditional roles make sense. They work. Boys tended livestock, drove wagons, plowed, and worked in the fields alongside their fathers. They simply had bigger muscles and broader reaches. Girls sewed, cooked, tended the children, the vegetable gardens, and even worked in the fields, perhaps hoeing corn. However, rare was the woman who plowed corn and truly worked the fields like a man. Rare, but not unheard of. Aunt Becky was the one who defied any role, rolled up her sleeves and got to it, whatever work she needed to get done. If she couldn't marry Steven, she'd do the work of a woman *and* the man she couldn't have. Which is why she was so well-equipped to take on her next challenge.

Her brother, Dan Cable and his wife were both ill in the spring of 1896. Dan, having mood issues for his entire life, was committed to a state hospital, while his wife was in a sanatorium sickbed suffering from Tuberculosis. Consumption. It was only fourteen years ago that the now-famous Dr. Robert Koch discovered that the wasting disease was actually caused by bacteria. *Mycobacterium tuberculosis.* What a long formal title! They just called it TB, or the White Plague, and it killed one out of every seven people in the United States and Europe. Some survived, but for many, the body was eaten away, the lungs no longer able to get enough air. Chest heaving, fatigue, coughing up blood ...a poor soul who was nowhere near any water, slowly drowned.

The situation did not go unnoticed.

"Poor Becky. She has to take care of those kids. Brother's in a hospital. You know, for the mind." Elijah Oliver said to his sister, Elizabeth.

"He did always go into those dark moods, even as a child."

"Mmm hmmm. And I heard the wife just died of her TB. Lungs just gave out. Coughed up all that blood just the night before. Wasn't even awake the last week or so. They left five kids. And look. Becky's out there tendin' the cattle, the crops, *and* those kids. A saint that one."

Despite the permanent rift that sprung with her father over the boy she loved, John Cable still passed on an exceptional work ethic to his daughter, and a lot of her spunk could also be credited to him. Thank goodness for that; she would need these traits the rest of her life.

How am I to tend this entire farm and take care of five children? How things work out... She sighed to herself. *God provides. But it is ironic isn't it? I don't even have time for marriage or my own family. Would Steven have been able to handle this?* She thought he would but...she put her hand up and waved it furiously as to if to swat a fly. *Just keep moving.*

Before *he was sent away,* as the whispers went, Dan and his sister, Becky, had bought the store they ran; it was a two-story frame home—the first frame home in the cove—made with lumber made from her father's mill. The store was on the lower floor, and the living quarters on the top.

Why not work at your father's mill? "Don't you remember? I did! That's where I cut off my calf almost clear through! See, here's the scar to prove it." Hiking up her simple calico day dress, there was a chunk of meat missing from Becky's calf, the result of an accident at the mill. She was simply working too fast, not paying attention as she should've been. Oh, she had bled! It took all the rags in the place to staunch the bleeding. Luckily, the doctor had his share of sewing needles and sewed her right up, while she watched, a bottle of whiskey quickly running dry in her shaking hands.

With an entrepreneurial spirit, in addition to her store, she wound up keeping boarders to make ends meet just a little faster, while also farming and watching over grazing cattle. Anything and everything to survive; she provided and even thrived. Becky was well-respected and sought after for advice on anything from sewing clothes to farming to the importance of wearing shoes.

Or not.

For she was frequently barefoot out in the fields, even when plowing with mules or herding cattle to the balds of mountain peaks. A neighbor and friend, John McCaulley, walked to church one Sunday, excited about his contribution to the local gossip. "Aunt Becky was barefoot again! And lo and behold, guess what happened?" He paused for effect, the others hanging on his words. What had happened to their Aunt Becky in her bare feet?

"Well. She had stepped on a sleepin' rattlesnake while walking to the sugar cove to check on her stock. You know? Becky's Sugar Cove, as she calls it, right up Mill Creek. Anyways, her reaction? Well...." he chuckled, "well, you know her! She said to that snake, 'you didn't hurt me old fellow, don't guess I'll hurt you!'" *That's our Becky!* "And she never took the head of a shovel to it. Like anyone else woulda done!"

"What're you all laughing at?" Aunt Becky strode up, in shoes, this being Church day. But anyone could tell she wasn't at her most comfortable.

"You!" they ribbed her, but loved her deeply. "You done forgave that rattlesnake! Who else woulda done that?"

"Y'all laughing at me?" She flew her head back and laughed with abandon. "Alright! I say, if you can laugh at yourself, you've got something."

They agreed, patting her on the shoulder, and the children giving her hugs. To Aunt Becky, children were very welcomed, and not just because they meant more hands on the farm. Lighter work was always cherished and sought after, and more children meant lighter work for sure. But she genuinely loved children, displaying a rare and special patience.

She taught her brother's five children to cook. She knew how the entire process worked. She plowed the fields, planted the seeds, gathered and ground the corn, and prepared the food, everything from cheesy grits with salt and butter to the lightest corn muffins in the cove. "Corn muffins can be heavy. Hockey pucks!" The children laughed at her comments. "But there's a way to make 'em lighter. Look here ...dump in more flour. And more sugar. The more flour the better."

And she taught them her methods of making clothing out of wool and flax. She was quite the seamstress, and always patiently lighthearted, showing the best stitches for dresses and another type for overalls. "They gotta last."

"My mother would've been grateful for Aunt Becky. And proud of her." Elijah Oliver often said of his cheerful and resourceful neighbor. "Thank goodness, Cades Cove has a new matriarch."

ᓚᓂᓕᔪChapter Elevenᔪᓂᓕᓚ

1890s

In the years following 1896, Becky Cable was still tending her fields, and raising her brother's children; she was just as spry and springy as ever. "Fresh air and good food," is what she preached. "Sleeping is good too. Those three things will give you a good life."

Elijah and the Oliver clan were still robust, but fewer. Mary "Polly" Oliver, the one who came to the cove as a small child, had died in May, 1892. Martha, the first Oliver born in the cove, in October 1864. Ruth in 1891. There was a child born in 1824, but he died right after birth. His name was George. Their mother and father had rarely spoken of him, but laid a flower and a prayer every single Wednesday and Sunday morning until their deaths. They were all together now, in the arms of heaven.

Elizabeth, Lazarus, Elijah and William Oliver remained.

Religion still reigned over their daily lives, and still constituted much of their social lives, yet Cades Cove residents remained practical as ever. There were three churches—the Primitive Baptist Church, the Missionary Baptist Church, and the Methodist Church. The one that most original members belonged to remained the Primitive Baptist

Church, which they visited every Sunday and multiple times a week.

John and Luraney's graves were never without heaps of flowers. Cove residents never just buried their dead, soon to be forgotten. No—stories, legends, and memories kept them front and center in the community, their graves were visited sometimes daily, but definitely two or three times a week, and their memories were passed down through the generations. Infant graves were rarely spoken of, but held the freshest flowers, and if marked, some of the most deeply etched stones. Legends, memories—whenever we want, we can transport ourselves back in time, to a smiling face, a familiar laugh. Smells of grandmother's homemade pies. Lathery soap and creamy pumpkin butter. The sounds of bare feet splashing in rocky creeks. *Ow!! We shoulda worn shoes!* What would father say? Well, we know what he'd say ...he'd quote somethin' from Ben Franklin. "In Truth, I found myself incorrigible with respect to Order, and now I am grown old and my memory bad, I feel very sensibly the want of it."

Memories. How we feel the want of it.

"How lucky are we?" Elizabeth Oliver often repeated to her brothers, especially when grouped together under the stand of thick trees on the Oliver homestead, where the eagles like to fly. "We all cross through here, our lives productive and we love each other fully. Stick together. Family is everything. Mama used to say that, remember? Yet, when we die and go to God, we still remain here on earth, in that important vessel of memories."

"Speaking of vessels, our vessel of the Lord, the Missionary Baptist Church—we're going to build our own building on Hyatt Hill."

"Why, in this little cove, does there need to be *three* churches?" They wondered aloud, yet again, for they knew the story very well of course. It's just that when thought upon, it was still incredulous that just a few hundred people would need the Primitive Baptist Church, the Missionary Baptist Church, the Methodist Church, and now, yet another branch of a church was held in a schoolhouse near Peter Cable's place because the Methodists also split apart. All this for around 120 households and 600-700 souls.

The men would stand in the middle of the cove and collectively discuss that "perhaps twenty-five is our limit, for no more than forty-odd people can agree on anything."

Remember that other split in the Baptists? They'd all lamented the split, especially John Oliver, though one side held to the belief that the age of accountability or salvation for Baptists was twelve years old. "Ironic" the son, William Oliver said sadly, "That us religious people interfere with one another over age." He shook his head. He knew he was right, following the Bible and what they'd been taught from young children, from his very own father, yet he muttered to himself, "Shame on all of us."

Yet, in the spirit of his father, he offered help. It wasn't taken, but still, he'd offered it. The desire for community peace overrode the strongest of faiths.

"My goodness! Hasn't it been fifty years since you all established the Missionary?"

"Yes, fifty years. A long time."

"I'll say."

"But now, our membership is about 100 members. Used to be around forty. So we need a bigger building! Either that, or we meet in the fields."

"Oh no, you can't do that. God's house is everywhere to be sure. But I see how you all need a building. Someplace to convene and worship in your own way."

As was the custom, the church members got together, chipped in for materials and got lumber from the mill to construct their church. It did take a while though. A longer time than they'd planned. Still, they persevered. Building important places, whatever the scale, takes special patience, and time.

That same scenario had been playing out since last year, in 1895 in Asheville, North Carolina, just over 120 miles away from the cove. The Vanderbilt family was hard at work; starting almost a decade ago when they began buying land, gathering materials, and overseeing the building of a very special home, albeit on a much grander scale. Two hundred and fifty rooms in the French Renaissance Chateau style, Biltmore House opened up on Christmas Eve, 1895.

"Look here! It says it has 250 rooms!" marveled Elijah, pointing to the newspaper in his hand.

"We already know that! They've been reportin' it for years."

Elizabeth rolled her eyes at her brother but had to admit a shared amazement. The residents of Cades Cove lived in log cabins and had ramshackle barns, smokehouses, and corncribs surrounding their homes. The Biltmore, they'd read all about it in the papers and in letters from home, was as far away from their own ways of living that it may as well have risen from the ocean itself. Still, they had striking similarities.

Both were situated in the strikingly beautiful Smoky Mountains, and had views that stirred both man and beast. Both had to rely on the land for game and growing food, and each had stocks of animals to sustain them. Both rustic cove

211

and gilded Biltmore housed very family-oriented folk. Large families and tight-knit people, cherished by both.

"We have one room to sleep all of us. Well, some of us go up in the loft, true. But they have thirty-five bedrooms! Forty-three bathrooms! Some of us have less acreage than that!"

"Well, we have unlimited bathrooms!"

"Unlimited?"

"Yeah, the trees!" Elijah laughed, ribbing his sister a bit. "We also have unlimited holes we can dig. Anywhere we'd like!"

"Goodness, Elijah! We have outhouses! We're not pigs!"

"Oink, oink!" He snorted. "Some of us are proud to be pigs."

"The pig of Cades Cove, everyone!" Elizabeth had told her friends of her brother's antics, and they teased him by taking him to the trough later that afternoon where they had placed his dinner plate.

"Girls, girls ...I'm a man. I'll eat anywhere!" And he proceeded to sit down by the trough and eat his food with his hands behind his back. The grown women squealed with horror as they watched the Oliver man eat, proud to be a pig.

They loved each other, these Olivers. They had all been born in the cove, but Elijah had crossed out of it for just a bit of a time. The son of John he certainly was, but he had his mother's grounded spirit as well. Born in the cove in 1824 in the little cabin his father had built, Elijah had moved out of the cove before the civil war.

Why'd you go? Well, I want to seek my own opportunities. Just to see what's out there. Know what I mean? I'd been in this cove my whole life, and ...I wanted to make more money. Took Mary Betty—you know I married one of the Lawson girls—and the kids and wanted a taste of city life. Just a small taste. Not like a big buffet or anything. I'm still a cove man at heart. And I was always comin' back. But a man's gotta fly every once in a while. Else he'll regret and start resenting. I wanted to see if I could stay away from farming. I love it, but it's hard on a man's back. But soon, very soon, the bigger town wasn't satisfying. My two lives and wishes got entangled. Oh, it was nice for awhile. Kinda like dessert everyday. That gets old though. You want to return to the meatloaf and potatoes and blueberries picked by hand and plopped into a pie. To pumpkins used as steppin' stones. Town life was us livin' in a house. But our home is here, where food and fire await my body and soul.

After the war between the states, Elijah returned to his food and fire in the cove, and he built his own homestead on some of his father's land; he named it: Oliver Place.

So many crossed over this very land. His dear and beloved father. Strong and loving mother, sisters and brothers. An infant, nobody mentioned, one day old.

Oliver's Crossing.

Like his parents, upon re-entering the cove and securing his homestead, he immediately got to work. Yet, this generation, as they all do, did things a bit differently. *Our own way.* They had more buildings than their parents. Made life easier, but at the same time, there was more to keep up with. Each generation built on and adapted to different times. Elijah had a springhouse to keep milk and butter cool. A bigger and better smokehouse to store and preserve hams, shoulders, and sides of deer and bear meat for an entire year, though they still ate mostly pork because it was easier to preserve than other meats. A corncrib to store enough for grinding portions of the crop to a meal to last until the next harvest. A barn to shelter the horses, the mules they used to plow the fields, numerous cows, and to shelter buggies, sleds and wagons.

Another new building emerged during this time period—a "stranger's room." Hospitality walked hand in hand with religion—help one's neighbor was the sign of the times—one that had been passed on, but which now looked a bit different.

"Fishermen are going to be in the cove next week. Would you be willing to put them up for a day or two?" The answer to those letters and inquiries was always yes, and thus, the cove residents enjoyed a reputation as being friendly and especially welcoming. The "stranger's rooms" were built on the front porches, or nearby the homestead, and became so popular that fishermen and travelers would come to actively seek out Cades Cove as a place with homey inns and lathery soaps with walnuts and honey. Food, fire, and warm company greeted one and all, which worked out for the cove inhabitants too. They received a little bit more money. And so much news! So much gossip! Every day brought a new fad or product, or foodstuff.

"So, you fish eh?"

"Yeah, I like that creek right by the road. It's teeming with lamprey, shiners, bass, and ...the stoutest trout I ever seen! But they can be tricky..."

After he waxed about fish for half an hour, to which Elijah patiently listened, the fisherman turned his attention to the cove man. "What do you grow here? Corn?"

"Indeed. Corn is our most important crop."

"Aren't you also the Deacon here at the Primitive Baptist Church?"

"I am," he replied humbly.

"So ...corn. I think you ship some of it to our parts, is that right? It's the sweetest I ever tasted!"

"Yes sir. On account of the soil."

"So important."

"It keeps us alive. Feed it to mules, horses, hogs, and chickens too."

"I never dealt with corn. ' Cept to eat it of course." He chuckled, then got serious. "I've been a fisherman all my life. How do you ...handle the corn?" He was genuinely curious. He never farmed, always fished. He didn't want to appear ignorant, but every man had his specialty these days.

"Corn. Ah, well, it's hauled in from the fields and dumped into the crib through the high hatch above the wagon. Let me show you..." And they went outside in the dusk, where Elijah Oliver pointed out his wagon. "Small portions come out through the little front door ...see there?"

"Still on the cob and in the shuck, you have to let it dry real well ...sufficiently to be ground into meal, chicken feed or to be fed to livestock. See here..." he took the fisherman around the side to the corncrib. "You cannot understand corn unless you get the entire process. It's like a thread to a quilt— if one thread is off, or comes loose, the whole thing falls apart."

The fisherman noticed that the corncribs were long and narrow structures with very low ceilings—the top only came up to his waist! "See here, this corncrib has spaces between the logs left open. That promotes air circulation and enhances dryin'. Corn shucking here is ...well, we make it fun. Here in the mountains, we have to make our own fun, you know?" He smiled. "It's a social event where we all get together and help out. Sing songs. Feast when it's all over. And the fellow finding a red ear of corn—very rare, mind you—gets to kiss a girl. Any girl he wants."

The young fisherman smiled. "I think I saw a red ear down by the edge of your very field. Right edging the creek." He winked at that.

Elijah smiled. "I'm married. I already got my red ear." He laughed. "But if you found it, I have a friend who has a daughter ...she loves trout."

Social life was as rich as ever, especially with more visitors bringing more news and happenings, and the usual harmony amongst the residents was on solid footing. Everything from harvesting the land and carrying out each season's specific chores, to the still largest influence of all—religious gatherings. School events were also very popular; holding spelling bees and special competitions for the students. Even adults had their own schools; singing schools where they learned to sing hymns in chorus style. There were writing schools for writing organized letters, all the better to write to friends and family and even place their own small piece here and there in newspapers and pamphlets. Weddings and funerals rounded out the social gatherings of the cove.

The old guard had faded away, and the new generation, who lived through the war and upheaval, raised their own children and roamed the cove performing the same chores as John and Luraney and their neighbors did just about seventy, eighty years ago now. Except with a bit more ease.

Elijah Oliver had built part of his cabin over a spring, which kept eggs, milk and butter cold. His wife, Mary Betty, of the respected and deep-rooted Lawson family, had taken over her mother-in-law's butter and soap recipes and continued the tradition of providing her neighbors with the wonderfully luxurious goods. There was nothing like soap with a little honey and some crushed walnuts! Took the grime of the hot sun and hotter fields right off.

Another family had piped water from a spring into their house directly to a homemade kitchen sink. The Mingus Mill was now up and running, east and south on the road that crossed between a few communities. Though the cove had its own Cable Mill, the Mingus Mill served travelers and those who left the cove on other business. Besides, there were plenty of customers to go around.

Despite improvements to homes, better food storage technology, and such, most people in Cades Cove still lived in a primitive fashion. Only two to three families piped water from springs to sink faucets inside their homes. There was certainly no electricity, no inside bathrooms, basic farm tools and only the clothes that were needed, nothing too luxurious save for Luraney's soap and butter recipes, now manufactured by Elijah's wife, Mary Betty. And that was just the way they liked it.

This generation *was* more progressive, embraced technology, and was open to new ideas, but at the same time, they pushed back against new ways of doing things that seemed to be very willing to chip away at their traditions. Think of women washing pots and pans, mostly outside in the creek, all their lives. They'd get together and chat about their children, neighbors, news and friends; they solved problems, vented their feelings and shared a common everyday life. And then there comes along a new way of washing dishes.

The cove women faced that very issue: 1886 saw the first dishwasher; hand-operated. The women—still young— did not embrace this machine, did not see much difference; *the pots and pans get clean don't they? Why fix something that ain't broken? Besides, it was a large machine ...where would we put it? Take up half the house! I don't think so.* But the youngest girls, though they'd never see one in their homes—not anytime soon anyhow—saw potential, and spoke of it to their mothers and aunts. *It would be a major difference—an hour saved here, an hour there, more time to sit in front of the fire weaving, or making dinner, or even reading a book. Perhaps we could even sit and talk more often!*

The mothers and aunts were sure that this was not the way to go. And they talked about it, while rinsing pots and pans in the creek. *Do you think this new generation has less of a work ethic? Or is it simply being more efficient? Are they slacking on hard labor or are they using their time more efficiently?*

As every generation toggles between the old and the new ways, the answer lies in the viewpoint: innovation or depletion of values? Mothers and aunts will answer one way. Daughters another. They laughed together, the issue unresolved, but all could agree on one thing: *Luraney would've said, it depends on the lens*

c⁄⁀Chapter Twelve⁀⁀

1900s

The Walker sisters strode up from Greenbrier one day to the Oliver homestead. "We've got to get together to help Matilda," ever the no-nonsense pair, they briefly greeted, then pleaded with Elijah, as Mary Betty was just coming down the porch steps. Elijah had taken the place as the patriarch of the cove; someone most everyone went to for advice. Even now, nothing could be done in the cove without the Oliver family being involved.

"Help Matilda? What's wrong? What's going on?" Elijah had heard of trouble in the Shields-Gregory household but did not yet know what news the Walker sisters brought. They were usually tending to their homestead which included the Little Greenbrier School, northeast of Cades Cove, where, since 1882, their father had built and run the school. Children would sometimes walk four to nine miles a day to attend classes.

"Matilda Shields Gregory's husband just deserted her! And their son!"

"When my sister uses a full name like that, well ...y'all know it's serious. Brings tears to my eyes!"

"Okay, Margaret and Louisa..." Elijah tried to calm the sisters, who just walked many miles to help their friend.

219

"Sit down here. Let me get you some chairs." He ran inside, pulled out two chairs onto the porch and said, "Tell me exactly what happened." Mary Betty brought them two jars of water as her husband remained standing against the timbered porch.

Louisa began. *He was bad news. Always angry. Must've come from the bad egg side...the one who fought with the Rebs and pretty much killed his daddy. Pointed out the house to them Rebs anyways. So, he may as well have killed him himself. Remember? And his reliable rifle Long Tom still in the family. Anyways* ... she returned to the issue at hand. *He just done up and left! For good this time. But first, he burned the house down! Right to the ground!*

Mary Betty held a hand up to her mouth in horror.

"Oh, don't fret too much now," Louisa said upon seeing Mrs. Oliver's reaction. "He told her and the boy to leave. He wouldn't have burned them. No. He ain't *that* bad. Just the house. And the barn. No animals either. The drink overcomes his soul. Too much drink. Poor Matilda." She shook her head in sorrow for her neighbor and friend. Took a sip of the nice cool water from the jar.

"Where are her brothers?"

"Oh, Elijah! I am sure they have their guns slung low, ready to sniff him out. They're like to kill him if they catch him."

"Poor Matilda. We must help her!"

In one day, Elijah, some other neighbors, and Matilda's brothers, unsuccessful in tracking down their errant brother-in-law and neighbor despite valiant efforts, hastily built a small log cabin for the poor, deserted woman and her son. Food was brought in that day. And every day for a month. *They're ours. We take care of our own.*

The eagle watched the progress—from what was just a pile of fallen logs, to a structure with a chimney and all. Smoke soon poured out of the stone chute and smells of food wafted upwards. A large crowd of people remained all day. The eagle's breast filled with something like hope. He didn't know why, but he felt the need to fly over to Henry Whitehead's place, who had just dug a hole and placed his wife inside. The man had cried, lifting his hands to the sky.

"A new century! Can you believe it?!" Excitement filled the air on this New Year's Eve. The men had their guns ready to shoot at midnight. Loaves of bread were stacked on the table inside the Oliver log cabin and children ran around the dark woods in their heavy clothes, mimicking and mocking all the animal sounds of the dead of night. They were never scared. Growing up in these parts, they knew how to shoot guns from practically their cradle days, and knew the woods and animals like they knew their faithful God. Though there was no snow on the ground, the air boasted a chill that cut through their mittens and hats. The cows were restless, the pigs paced their pens. The eagle was safe in his nest, but awake, listening to the anticipation of the humans below.

The 125 households and 708 men, women, and children of Cades Cove celebrated the new year, the new century. 1900. The old guard was well entrenched in their use of their mills, sawed lumber, springhouses, and other such progress. The younger generation talked more and more of dishwashers and elevators. And electricity, which seemed most practical. Four schools, three churches. The entire cove converted into farm fields and homesteads. Roads. Fences. Animals everywhere.

The mountains provided an ever-safe refuge from invaders, both human and machine. But try as they might, the tree-lined, gently sloping peaks could not stop the world around them from encroaching closer and closer. Mountains are forced to change shape by nature's wrath and processes. Wind, water, all combined to sculpt their faces from sharp noses to gentle, calm slopes as they aged. It's the opposite for human aging. Forced changes in humans are fraught with steepened features, a chiseling away of once-peaceful emotions; it's when everyone leans on one another especially hard, and it's when denial hardens into a thick plaster: *they can't tell us how to live! They can't come here! This is our land!* It's those unseen, or rather, unacknowledged forces of aging that can kill at any time.

"He's changed Matilda's life!"

"They went to the Justice of the Peace at 10:00 p.m. after the fields were tended and Matilda could get the stew going in the pot. For something to eat when they got home...*you know,* one of the Tipton boys said with a wink.

"Oh hush!" Louisa Walker waved her hand in the air as if to push him away. The Walker sisters had walked to the cove the very next day after the late-night wedding.

"What's with these weddings in the cove being late at night?"

"It's the only time we have to celebrate. Days are taken up with fields and animals. We eat dinner. Bathe. Only then are we acceptable to attend a wedding."

"Hmmph. That's not how we did it in our day."

"Well, you two never married." It was pointed out to the Walker sisters.

"And we never will! We like being our own bosses."

"It is tough for women. We would have to obey our husbands."

"In your case, Louisa and Margaret Walker, I believe your husbands would have to obey *you!*" Elijah exclaimed with a hearty laugh. It was good-natured of course. Elijah had a good sense of humor, yet was always respectful. But the sisters looked at each other and smiled.

Louisa whispered to her sister: *He's right.*

The eagle was still watching as Henry Whitehead had risen from his wife's grave. Grieving, but ever the pragmatist, he looked up and saw the large bird, sighing deeply. *Whatever goes on in that creature's life, he still had to eat, preen, and seek a mate. Life doesn't stop for grief.* He walked home, his heart in a freefall, yet at the same time— maybe in a few months or so—he saw the practicality of having to marry again. For Henry Whitehead was just left with three small daughters to raise all on his own, not to mention working his farm and homestead. He needed help. Quickly. He needed a wife.

Though there were plenty of people around, pickings for wives were slim. The right age, temperament...it was difficult with so few to choose from. Matilda was nice, and had just been abandoned. She was hardworking. Why Gregory had run off on a Shields girl, he didn't know. He'd heard rumors of course. Nothing could happen around here without some gossip. They just hadn't gotten along, some said. But others pointed to too much moonshine. Way too much. To the point where he changed into a monster. Matilda, as far as he knew, was sweet natured, cooked, kept a clean home, and was a loving mother. Whatever Gregory's problem was with his wife—or with himself—Henry knew with instinctual clarity that any issues would not transfer over to their relationship of which he had high hopes.

He began slowly, walking over to see how she fared. *How's the house holding up? Any leaks? Chimney smoking well? I like bricks better than stone. This youngin' of yours is growing so strong!* Tousled his hair. Sweet, good-natured boy. *Do you have enough food? Your garden looks well-tended.*

For her part, she already knew that Henry was a nice, young widower. Hard working, had good land, three young daughters and came from a good family. He was kind. And didn't drink moonshine. *The house is wonderful, thank you.* And repeated: *I can't thank you enough for your help with it. I know you put together the chimney, with bricks no less ...it's nice and tight. I agree about the bricks ...I like them better than stone too. Thank you for your kindness, Henry. Let me show you some carrots. The radishes are coming in nicely, see here? Would you like to stay for dinner? Bring over your girls ....*

Courting was quick, and he married Matilda, blending their families—his three daughters and her small son. A family of six who all moved into a great log home from logs sawn square at a nearby mill. A tight-fitting corncrib was also built, with hardly any spaces left to fill in, yet leaving sufficient air circulation for proper drying. Henry was a master craftsman for sure, known the cove over for his fine work.

Corners of their home and outbuildings were near-perfection, most of the interior logs, ceiling joints, and boards were hand-planed lumber, and were so smooth, no splinter ever got under their rough skin. Their home was peaceful. No moonshine here. The cove men and women abstained from moonshine for the most part—something the surrounding communities—especially Chestnut Flats—did not share. Oh, they partook a bit, special occasions, definitely during childbirth, some Saturday evenings while visiting. But overall, the drink was not a major vice. They always had to rise early to tend the fields. Drinking made a crop die faster than a dead pig rots in the sun. And God was always watching; they'd do anything not to disappoint Him.

Chestnut Flats didn't care too much about such things; figured they'd work it out when they arrived in Heaven. If they did go to Heaven. *Go to Heaven for the weather, but Hell for the company.* But for the cove folks, they knew it didn't work that way, preferring to make for a smooth, clear, God-sanctioned passage. *Funny,* Matilda thought to herself while wrapped in a quilt by the fire, chatting with her new husband, *who would've thought that the devil's moonshine would save me from a life of misery? Blessings come in strange packages.*

⟨♪Chapter Thirteen♪⟩

1900-1936

They began as 708 people in the new century, watching as major shifts occurred in their bustling mountain society; they saw them even though people living through events day to day normally don't see such shifts until long afterward. Hindsight is both useless and powerful. Humans either rue the day or learn the lessons. The people of Cades Cove were simple mountain folk, but they were far from ignorant. Increasingly, their conversations turned to the lumber companies moving into Eagle and Hazel creeks, just north and south of the cove's still prosperous fields. Neighboring Catalochee's population numbered over 1200 now, and all communities began expanding.

"Funny. It took us forever to get mail. The Rebs never wanted our land, just our livestock and crops. Chestnut Flats folk only seem to want other people to fight, and the moonshiners bypassed us."

"Well, we aren't known to imbibe. We are their worst customers."

"Yeah, but now these lumber companies and the roads are well-traveled ...and now they're all talking about the park."

"Funny. I agree. What changed? This land's been here forever. We've been living in relative peace for a hundred years just about. Why are they interested in us now?"

What did change to make this secluded valley in the middle of the Smoky Mountains such sought-after land? And, could they really remove them from their own land? The land they've held for generations?

It would take another thirty years and another generation or two to answer those questions. By then, sixty-seven percent of the area would be cut down by logging companies. Unaware and ignorant, the cove residents were not. They could see these changes surrounding them for years, and they'd heard all the whispers and increasing warnings. Heeded them, yes. What to do about it? That was still as up in the air as the clouds shrouding the pleats of the mountains.

"It gave me a great job that loggin' company. But it destroyed our forests, our land..."

"It's going to destroy our way of life."

"Going to? It already has! They've been talking about the national park for just about a decade now!"

"Why are they even interested in our land? Most never even knew we existed!"

"Well, Kephart did ...he wrote about mountain life. What was the name of his book again?"

"Our Southern Highlanders."

"Yeah. All of us moonshiners!" they laughed. "But he was honest. Real. That's us. Well, it's not really us in the cove ...it's a lot of folks around us though. Chestnut Flats..."

"Ugh, them folks are something else. Always fightin.'"

"Always drinkin' and pissin' away at that moonshine."

"But we are just simple mountain folk. God-fearing. Neighborly. And we just want to be left alone."

"Farm prices are lower. Moonshiners all around us. Lots of younger folk have left for jobs, electricity…to the bigger towns. They live comfortably there."

They thought about the vivid truths of change.

"More than half of us already got that government money and left. That leaves just about half of us." They repeated. "Half! Who's left? Who's going to fight for us?"

Months, years. Eagles continued to soar, higher now, as if surveying the land from an even further vantage point. Surely they couldn't see the details as well from so far away. Seasons came and went. The same conversations.

They looked at one another and sighed. "True. We only got about 540 people left. And more of us goin' and packing up as we speak…"

"There's only one person who can do it. Fight for us. The great-grandson of our patriarch, our founder…"

"Ah, yes. He learned from the best."

"That would be John W. Oliver, of course."

"Oliver. Absolutely, the only one who can do it. That entire family all crossed through here. *Oliver's Crossing.* That's what we shoulda named it."

"True. We've been calling it that amongst ourselves for years."

"Good people. None of us would've been here without 'em."

"Probably not. That's true."

"Maybe some of us woulda found our way here ...eventually. But John was first. He paved the way. Took a stand. Them Indians were here, but he said, no here's my chance at my own farm. A chance to be the man I always wanted to be. And he moved his little family into the bowl of plenty. Built a homestead, a farm ...taught all of our grandfathers what to do, how to survive the cove. John Oliver started it all. Bravery took a stand and won."

"Took a stand ..." they were silent, knowing the fight ahead.

"Now it's time for *us* to take a stand. With no less than John Oliver's brand of bravery."

"Sad to say, I think it's our last one."

"Cades Cove's last stand." They looked at one another with strong and steady eyes.

"Let's hope we win."

The great-grandson, John W. Oliver, was born in the cove in 1878, growing up under chestnut and maple trees, his biscuits saturated with his great-grandmother's pumpkin butter, and learning all he needed to know about survival. He did leave the cove to attend college, having received a solid education in the cove school. After receiving his degree, the "new" John Oliver arrived fresh from Maryville College, settling down in the cove on July 16, 1900. By January, 1901, he was teaching at the school where he earned twenty-three dollars his first month. What did he buy with that very first paycheck?

On Sunday, Nancy Ann (Whitehead) and I rode horseback all the way from Maryville through the flats of Chilhowee Mountains to Cades Cove a distance of twenty miles without ever dismounting from our horses. It was a cold blue day but our hearts were warm for each other. I had on the first whole suit of clothes I ever owned. I bought them on Saturday January 26, 1901 with the first money I ever earned teaching school at twenty-three dollars per month. They cost me eight dollars and fifty cents. We were twenty-two years old and not married. We were married September 4, 1901.

John Oliver returned to the cove in full force, teaching, and tending his land.

"After popping in and out for a few times, he settled here for good and became kind of the ...progressionist for the cove." The others soon realized just what it meant for this young man to have returned to his home, bringing with him a unique knowledge of the workings of the world.

"He sure did."

"What's a progressionish?" One of the children asked. Deemed old enough to understand and even to be taught such things, they indulged the child.

"Well, as a progression*ist*, he implemented vaccinations for animals to prevent common diseases and conditions, introducing a "thoroughbred Aberdeen Angus bull" which bred with virtually every cove cow, resulting in superior stock."

"I seen that bull." the child exclaimed. No big deal. They'd seen such breeding their entire lives. It was part of nature. "He's the biggest animal I ever seen."

No small feat breeding with almost every cow in the cove, for there were many—"he serviced over eighty-four cows."

The child whistled. "That's a lot. No wonder we always have calves."

"John also upgraded hogs with a Berkshire boar in 1914, used incubators for chicken eggs and new methods of farming such as new seeds, and machinery. New varieties of fruit trees were imported, upgraded the bees (triple the production of honey) and 'crusaded for better health care'."

They were silent, thinking back to the Oliver family and this "new" Oliver who learned so much at college and seemed to be able to see the future.

"He sure is honoring his great grandfather who— remember—settled here with nothing but his wife, a little daughter, and one on the way."

"He made it through that first winter and every one thereafter, with his own two hands. Cleared land. Built a house. An entire homestead. Nobody else to help. Now, *that's* a man."

John W. Oliver didn't yet know what the future held ...didn't he? He knew he felt something deep in his bones, and it bothered him to no end. It was one thing to teach the youth in the cove and to introduce better livestock. It was something else altogether to know that he would never get to teach his own grandchildren under the maple trees and in the creeks of Cades Cove. *A way of life is dying. Progress is good in a lot of ways. But both empire and tiny mountain communities are organisms. Like living creatures, they pass through stages: from early days to growth spurts, from maturity to decline, and then, to the inevitable end.*

There should be someone to whom to pass on all this knowledge, John lamented. Though he was confident he would have people to pass on mountain life's unique lessons—his own offspring and fellow neighbors and friends, he was growing equally confident that those people would have to learn in a brand new place, away from the forests, creeks, fields, and soaring eagles.

Under a harsh sun, some of the final harvests came to ripeness. Wheat, oats, field greens, peas and lettuce. Potatoes. And of course, the mighty corn harvest. They worked hard and still were wishing that all could remain the same. But the outside world drove itself more and more inside the cove, so much so that on September 26, 1915, right during the turmoil of WWI, the cove saw its very first automobile, a 1912 Cadillac, drive down the road and into the southeast's farmland. How amazing! Oh, they'd been enticed with serious plans for a railroad to be built in the general area for years; the world war had put a halt to those plans. But now, a car! The Shields family was the first to be driven around the cove that day by a family friend, Jack Fisher. Thereafter, Jack Fisher was especially welcomed in the cove. *Just please be sure to come with your automobile,* the children would plead.

This back and forth dialing kept up a frantic pace between one side of fascination and progress and the other side of maintaining prideful clinging to a way of life that they knew was dying. They just couldn't face it. Not yet. Not ever.

Automobiles, the expensive telephone, more and more rules and regulations. Taxes. Bigger and more competition, and tougher times for selling their grains and goods. *Government interests encroaching on their land.*

The last stand of Cades Cove had to happen now.

In 1929, John W. Oliver, the descendant of the original John and Luraney Oliver bloodline, was tasked to fight for the cove's people in a spirited and bitter eminent domain battle with the government. *They want our land! And why? To make a national park? The greater good of the people, they say. We will all benefit. All of us? Not us! Besides, we'd heard that before. Tryin' to butter us up and knock us into yesterday, so they can seize it all today. We know exactly what's goin' on. We've been talkin' about it for years here in our fields.*

But we have a plan.

It began in the Tennessee State Government and ended up in the State's Supreme Court.

It took six years and three appeals, an all-out effort to preserve home and heritage.

Showing up to court for each and every hearing, John was sure that during the last one, he had made a difference. He spoke very well and became more and more comfortable before the court. College and then teaching might have prepared him with rhetorical and public speaking skills, but the cove had prepared his heart with the most exquisite of passions—the idealism, goodness, and rich history of Cades Cove and its people.

"It is what God wanted." He began, his hands sweating, but his voice firm. "But let's not focus on faith. Here are the facts."

He took a breath. Everything was riding on his words.

The geology of the Smoky Mountains and our secluded cove dates back to the Lower Cambrian Age. He was glad he had listened in his science and geology classes. He needed all the authority he could muster. Straightening his tie, he continued, "with elevations averaging 1,750-2,000 feet. Such lush, rich soil could only come about because of its limestone base which retains lots of water, so much in fact that even in dry seasons, the ground is moist enough for bumper crops. That is why we settled here. We could make a living, provide for ourselves and others… We were useful. We *are* useful. Ask anyone around here about our sweetest of corn. Or my great-grandmother's soap and butter."

The Judge prodded him on. "Tell us about your people."

"Well, you know no story is complete without our own Aunt Becky." he began, well aware that her reputation was known even here in the State Supreme Court building.

The judge smiled and nodded his head. "I know Aunt Becky."

"You'd be taking Aunt Becky away from her land. I don't know if you know this, but once, some years ago, she became gravely ill. Thought she was dying before the next moon was full. Oh, she realized her condition—but she is stubborn you know …never would acknowledge she was sick. So, she summoned John McCaulley, one of our neighbors, to build her coffin. She paid him with wool socks, which she herself had made. She is a great seamstress."

"Indeed she is." The judge agreed, smiling, his hands folded and leaning back in his big black leather chair.

"Well, because of her solid foundation as a member of the cove's own Missionary Baptist Church in Cades Cove, Aunt Becky prepared to meet her God. She was ready to depart the cove, her home."

Everyone was silent. Even the audience, who either knew Aunt Becky or had heard of her. The few who didn't sat in awed silence.

"Well, Aunt Becky—she was pretty sick by now—gazed to the opposite bank of Mill Creek—she could see it from her window—and experienced a vision of Jesus Christ himself extending uplifted arms to her."

"My goodness ...I hadn't heard she...." The judge was visibly moved. He hadn't heard this news at all.

"But, just like that, the vision ended. And our Aunt Becky recovered and is still living a very productive life."

The judge visibly relaxed.

John continued. "And you know what she said?"

"What?" asked the judge, after John paused to collect himself.

"Jesus just isn't ready for me yet."

The courtroom erupted in laughter. What a fire spark Aunt Becky was and she wasn't even present!

"Your Honor," after the laughter had died down, one and all nodding their heads in joy at the spunky old aunt. "I simply relay these stories to implore to you ...you are taking away real people. Memories. A way of life!"

"Okay, let's hear more." the judge commanded. John was enthused. If he could keep talking, and relaying stories, perhaps he'd sway the judge...

"We are fully aware that the government wants our land in order to establish that national park. The Great Smoky Mountains National Park is what they want to call it. Oh, it sure is beautiful, we love it like no other place on earth. There is a magic to the breeze as you stand in the middle of the corn. You can't see it, but you can feel it brush your cheek as you walk up a quiet creekside trail and watch the eagles soar. Children roam free, allowed an imagination. You can't really get that in the bigger towns. At Maryville College, I sure learned a lot, but the creativity, the problem solving within the cove's isolation is like no other ...like when a horse is suddenly injured two miles out, or when the fields look a bit dry, or even when there's only you and a horse and wildland and you gotta build a house ...solving problems in a town just isn't as meaningful. Good, honest work makes for grit and God working hand in hand. Human and beast alike stay and make their home here. A warm valley under a smiling sun, hugged by Mother's mountains."

The judge looked thoughtful; perhaps he wasn't even paying attention anymore, the imagery of John's words scratching a vivid likeness onto the very spot on the wooden podium where he now stared.

"But it's *our* home, Your Honor." John's voice, more powerful now. The judge looked up.

"It's the Shields' home. Lawsons. The Ogle's home. The Cable and Tipton's home. The Jobe and Oliver homes. Goodness ...George Washington Carter Shields—of the Shields family—is a cripple for life! And we all take care of him. He was wounded in the Battle of Shiloh, but he married and moved back to Cades Cove, bought property...where else can he be productive? And accepted? You may think farm and field is no place for a crippled man ...the big towns and cities would be better, right? They've got resources. But fresh air, neighbors, a special harness for his horse, and his family having deep roots in the land ...his Sunday church gatherings, picnics where we go to him, and move his chair under the maple tree for the afternoon ...there's no accounting for that anywhere else. He'd die if he were moved." The judge looked down, looked about to say something. John was scared he'd ask him to stop.

"I pray you let me continue ...." John pled.

Seeing the judge nod, he did just that.

"Colonel Hamp Tipton—another example. He owned property in the Cove. Though he, himself, lived in nearby Tuckaleechee Cove, he built a house in the early 1870s. Miss Lucy and Miss Lizzie, his daughters, lived there both taught school in the Cove. They had an apiary—a bee gum stand; honey was made; had a smokehouse and woodshed; and across the road, a double pen corncrib, larger than average, with a driveway through the center. Behind the corncrib was a cantilever barn. Where else can you find these things? Sure, they're around, but ours...ours are special."

My goodness, he was talking fast! He just had to get all these stories out. They couldn't just die away with the wind...

Focus John, he told himself "The way we build, the way we feed ourselves. We live differently. You may not see that ...don't most of us have farms? Corncribs? Sure, lots of folks around here do. But I tell you, Your Honor, ours are special. I can't explain it, but just know that ours are one of a kind. If you take us over—if the government takes us over—that way of life is gone. That would be a tragedy. Not just for us. For our unique American culture."

"Okay, we are almost in recess. One more?" The judge told John.

"Gosh ...there's so many." John wracked his brain to come up with the most persuasive memories. "The Sparks family, the Powell's, the Myers ...Absolum Abbott Sr., who was a Baptist Preacher. The Burchfields ..." Oh, he was rambling on ...too many families to honor. *They are in our hearts even if not spoken aloud.* Had to get back on track with the stories.

"The hearty Shields family again ..." boasted John, "...one of their large brood from way back—he was a gunsmith and scout for the Lewis and Clark Expedition. Yessir, that was more than a decade back before my great-grandfather, the first John Oliver, even came to the cove in 1818. But still ...goes to show what kind of people we come from."

"And, Joshua Jobe—who came here with my father—his son, Abraham Jobe, attended Andrew Johnson, our President, on his deathbed. That was a long time ago too. But these are the kinds of people we come from. And the kind of people the cove *produces!*" His voice rose and he became emboldened. Time was running out.

"Your Honor. We produce not only grains and corn. Cades Cove, Tennessee produces the most kind, service-oriented, God-fearing, neighborly people one can find. One of us attended a President. Many of us fought in the war and *all* of us suffered alongside our country. We endured hardships ...never taking from anyone! We keep to ourselves and take care of ourselves. Yet we are part of the bigger nation too. What more can America want? We love our country. We fought for it."

John cleared his throat. Took a breath, tamping down the lump in his throat. *One last chance to pour my soul out for our beloved home.*

"Please ...I plead with you, Your Honor, on my own behalf, and on behalf of all the people and memories of Cades Cove, please reject that America can take this way of life away."

His spirited fight against Tennessee's state government ended in the State Supreme Court's square, cold, white marble building.

"Six years it's been ..." the judge announced to the crowded courtroom with his slow Tennessean drawl, "A compromise will allow all residents of Cades Cove to remain in their homes with a lifetime lease."

"At least there's that." John W. Oliver, defeated after a fight lasting longer than the Civil War, walked down the steps of the courthouse and caught a wagon back to Cades Cove. He looked at it through a different, sadder lens as he arrived through the mountain pass and into the vast clearing. No matter how hard he tried to hold them back, he shed thick tears at the sight of the crops, still as well-tended as ever. The homesteads and smoking chimneys dotting the perimeter of the entire fertile bowl. Fewer people milled about though. Fewer animals. Actually, it did seem smaller. *When had that happened?* The younger generation was making their way in the world, with all the cove's values intact. The problem was, they were making their way in the world ...somewhere else. *They will never come back.* And then, a moment of clarity for John. *Even if the government weren't building a national park, they'd still never come back.* In the end, the country's progress had taken their past, and now, their future.

Alas, John W. Oliver lost his last stand, but fought as valiantly as the mightiest hero. He rocked on the front porch for many a night after walking down those courthouse steps, thinking of his future. His past. The betrayal of the government. Because the government and their word, Oliver had always respected; but now he found it was all worthless.

They told us we could stay for our lifetimes! But the government seized our homes anyway. They didn't even let the ink dry on the dang papers! Eminent domain. The right of the government to take private property for public use, with payment and compensation, of course, all for the public good. The greater good.

Five million dollars of John D. Rockefeller's money was raised for this and—had they truly had a choice?—a lot of residents willingly sold. We already know that. It is done. But some did not sell, and spurred on by me—the Oliver savior—he laughed sardonicall ...Savior. Ha! ...spurred on by me, friends, neighbors, we all raised what little money we had, hired a lawyer, raised our defense, and fought for years. Six years. I spoke up in that drafty courtroom when I was as nervous as a squirrel in a bear den. But I still spoke for everyone in that courtroom. And they promised us we could stay. We got it in writing! Broken promises. Who cares about money? We want our land and our way of life ....

Alas, we lost...

William Howell Oliver, another descendant of the original John, had come up the gravelly walkway to see John W. Oliver sitting in his porch chair. Rarely idle prior to this ordeal, John sat in that chair on the porch more and more. Remembering. Wondering. Regretting.

Ticked off.

"As if forcing us off our land isn't enough! As if this Great Depression wasn't enough! Stock market crashed. People are linin' up in lines just for bread. And we grow enough for us and everyone else! Yet, they're throwin' us out. Don't make sense. Forcing families from their homes, in which we merely intended to live out our days, is especially cruel in this day and age! Bad enough they took our land ...but they *promised* we could stay for our lifetimes. Ticked is not the word." He banged the chair's arm, suddenly rising and letting it rock back and forth all by itself. He walked down the two porch steps to the walkway. Hands on his hips, looking out.

"I agree, John," William said quietly.

Oliver's Crossing was gasping for air, all the while knowing it was futile.

"Even those very few detractors conceded that you fought with courage and tenacity in trying to save our homes and way of life," William said.

"Thank you," replied John, and then looked to the west. "It's a death. It feels like the worst death of all. Mother and Father are here...so many of our own. Jobe. Tipton. Shields ...Everyone is here."

William Howell Oliver nodded and hung his head. He was no longer embarrassed about shedding tears, which flowed gently. "This land, our churches especially...." he could not hold back and a torrent of tears came.

"The creek ...no competition ...I can shed more tears than all the creeks flowing..." His head hung in his hands, body shaking in angry sorrow; John grabbed his shoulder in knowing and shared sadness. The two men embraced one another, sharing in the deepest of sorrows for what they had lost. Suddenly, they heard a loud noise.

"Oh." William said, taking a deep breath, releasing John, and wiping his face. "There's the eagle." The two men watched as the bird perched on a tree just to the north of the porch. "Look, it's looking at us."

"It sure was squawking loud. And it landed there with such a crash ...what was that all about?"

The two men wondered. And then, the eagle took off, soared again, making its way to the cemetery, and, unseen to the two men, the eagle landed on the ground between two mounds that still had towers of fresh flowers covering the entire graves. It bowed its head in respect and remained there until the sun kissed the tops of the tree-lined peaks. On the other side of the peaks, the moon's face was crowning.

"John," William sighed, knowing exactly where the eagle was headed, "it seems like we are selling our dead."

On Christmas Day 1937, John W. Oliver moved the last of his household goods from his home in the cove. It was a bitterly cold day and traces of snow were falling. The cove was essentially empty, but John's mind was racing and full of emotions. He looked around one last time. The hum of the creek, the fields, now smaller than ever, the deer, the maple trees, the largest and broadest of chestnuts, the homesteads that dotted the landscape ...the church steeple …the graveyards with beloved souls resting quietly beneath fresh flowers covered with a light dusting of snow. The cold air was especially sharp this morning. He noticed that the eagle made many restless appearances throughout the day.

It was time to say goodbye.

My cove, my home may be empty, but in my mind, there are many people whose spirits remain. They represent the richest inheritance and finest examples of the cove's existence as an organized community since 1818. John wrote a final entry into his diary notes. He didn't have to try to remember this sad day—it would sear into his memory forever. But he wrote one last sentence of hope, something he wished he actually felt just then, but knowing it would be a long, long time before he actually did feel anything resembling an uplifting thought. He wrote, slowly: *As long as their memory remained alive, the community of Cades Cove would never die.*

Chapter Fourteen

1937—THE NATIONAL PARK

There were twenty-one families left in the cove. The rest of humanity was in the midst of its second world war. Matilda and Henry Whitehead remained, living very happily together in the well-built home tucked away in the southwest corner of Cades Cove. In 1939, The Little River Lumber Company finished cutting timber in the nearby Tremont area. No more mail by 1940—so many people had sold or fled and so few remained that the Post Office closed October 31, 1947.

There's not enough mail to be delivered. We will close the route. But just because there were not enough people living here anymore to deliver and receive mail, didn't mean there was a lack of people around. Far from it. On September 2, 1940, President Franklin Roosevelt was at the Rockefeller Memorial at Newfound Gap, dedicating the Great Smoky Mountains National Park to a very large crowd who couldn't wait to drive the road to the now-historical site of Cades Cove. To see how those people really lived. President Roosevelt opened the park with heartfelt remarks:

Newfound Gap—September 2, 1940 at the Dedication Ceremony of Great Smoky Mountains National Park.

Here in the Great Smokies, we meet today to dedicate these mountains, streams and forests to the service of the millions of American people. We are living under governments that are proving their devotion to national parks.

"D'ya hear? The President mentioned us!" A younger Tipton boy heard all about it at school that day. His family, along with most of the cove residents had moved out, pocketed their government checks, and settled into neighboring towns. They bought land, homes, and re-settled their children into other schools. Life went on. Just not their *way* of life. They were in bigger towns now where they never saw any eagles at all. Everything seemed to be moving so fast.

The pioneers stood on their own feet, got their own game and fought off their own enemies. In time of incident or misfortune, they helped each other. In time of Indian attack, they stood by each other. Today we no longer face Indians and hard and lonely struggles with future. But also, we have grown fit in many ways.

That September dedication day brought a bright dawn, the leaves displaying their first hints of bronze and copper, beckoning a meaningfully solemn fall in the cove. All former residents, wherever they now were in the larger world, recalled with warmth, the long, sweaty harvest days, the deep sleeps and cold creeks, and the apple cider made from the richest, most luscious apples they'd ever eaten.

It is not in every case easy or pleasant to ask men of the nation to leave their homes and women of the nation to give their men to the service of the nation. But the men and women of America have never held back even when it has meant personal sacrifice on their part if that is sacrifice for the common good.

The winds that blow through the wide sky in these mountains. The winds that sweep from Canada to Mexico, from the Pacific to the Atlantic have always blown on free men. We are free today. If we join together now—men, women and children—and face the common menace as a united people, we shall be free tomorrow.

And so, to the free people of America, I dedicate this park.

The birth of the national park marked the death of the Cades Cove community. Those remaining saw the last school sessions in 1943-44. On January 22, 1941, the Walker Sisters—holdouts for so long, but wise enough to understand the lost fight—sold their property to the government for inclusion in the new national park for $4,750, along with a stipulation that they be *"allowed to reserve a life estate and the use of the land for and during the life of the sisters."* The sum was less than the actual value, but the sisters were so entrenched in their mountain way of life that they kept saying "I'd never part with this grandest of scenery!"

"The President visited us!" The sisters would proudly state to their remaining neighbors. "He spoke so well ...of honor and sacrifice, and duty to one's country...well, we seen we couldn't win." They would sadly relay the story and their reasoning, never without a heavy, heavy sigh. "And ...oh it pains me to even say it ...but we was defeated. We sold."

"Well, you sisters sure have kept our way of life, even if hangin' by a thread. We're grateful for that. That's the sticky rub ...it's not just that it was our land, it's what we did on it. We lived our lives on this land. We made it better." They'd all nod their heads, in remembrance.

We sure had a good thing goin' here.

The government and park, for their part, did want to preserve their way of life and worked hard to preserve the buildings, the stories of the cove, and the culture. People were fascinated by this glimpse into a secluded and isolated, but bustling and successful, slice of Appalachia. That fascination found its way to the Saturday Evening Post in 1946. They "published a feature article that highlighted the Walker Sisters' traditional lifestyle, which subsequently led to a steady stream of tourists to their farm. There was so much interest, and it was all quite overwhelming, that Margaret and Louisa wrote a letter to the Superintendent of the Park, in 1953."

To the Supertendant of the Great Smokie Mountain National Park

Dear Sir

I have a request to you Will you please have the Sign a bout the Walker Sisters taken down the one on High Way 73 especilay the reason I am asking this there is just two of the sisters live at the old House place one is 70 years of age the other is 82 years of age and we can't receive so many visitors We are not able to do our Work and receive so many visitors, and can't make sovioners to sell like we once did and people will be expecting us to have them, last year we had so many people it kept us buisy from Sun up till sun down besides our own work We haven't bin feling very well this winter can't do much at our best. I write poems to sell but cant write very well I use to write of winter but I havent bin able to do much for the 2 last ones My Brother is in the Hospital and cant stay with us much We mis his help We have a Grant Nephew and his wife with us now There was 5 of us living here when we began to receive visitors and we enjoyed meeting so many nice people from different places from every state in the union and many out side, some of them came every time they came to the park, there was more of us and we were more able to care for things, they bought things from us and made it easier to have spinding money. they buy things yet if we was abel to fix them but it is to confining on us now with no more help if we get to feeling better or get till we can receive them a gain we may want to receive them a gain but we want to rest a while it is to much work for us now. Come visit us if you have time.

Very Respectively

The Walker Sisters

Margaret and Louis

The years toiled on and the special way of mountain cove life lingered on its deathbed. The Primitive Baptist Church was "unwilling to disband and maintained membership into the 1960s." But the other churches disbanded...there just weren't enough people. And the souls who remained were shadows of their former selves. They would simply worship under God's blue skies, or wherever He replanted them in the world.

More and more just gave in, sold, and moved away. Very few residents signed life-leases to remain on their land for the rest of their lives. But if they did, they paid a price— some were forced out anyway, via a government's stealthy ways. Some were given less money for their land and their freedoms were encroached. They had to live by rules set by the government's National Park Service. There were hunting and trapping restrictions, and timber cutting needed permitting. They could no longer do as they wished with their own land—*ugh*—they kept forgetting *...it isn't our own land anymore!*

But don't tell that to Aunt Becky. She remained, tending her fields in her bare feet and living life the way she always had; seeing the Great Smoky Mountains National Park come into existence, and remaining here until her death in 1940. She was 96 years old.

Many folks returned for her burial in the Cable Cemetery, which is, one of the eulogies explained, "Adjacent to the field she formerly plowed and near the site of the Cable School which she enabled."

"The Preacher spoke for the small crowd amassed on that day. They rejoiced her memory and spoke about the old days. How far away those days seemed! *When we ran barefoot all day long ...when we milked the cows at dawn and picked blueberries... When we climbed mountains all day, and rang the bugles for the Rebs! We hunted rabbits, and played in the creeks all summer. Harvested every crop for miles! Hard work. Indeed, but didn't it feel fun? Did it really feel like work? They agreed it did not. It felt like ...life. It was simply life. It moved on each and every day. Only when we smelled Mama's stew did we run for home. Under the moonlight. Under the eagle's eye.*

"How very appropriate that as her soul soared to her final Cove of happiness and fulfillment, her body is now assimilated into Cades Cove, a place synonymous with the name Aunt Becky Cable." The Preacher made his final speech and quieted, and the church bell was rung, scaring off the eagle that was perched on its steeple.

They bowed their heads in respect for the Aunt of Cades Cove.

The Oliver and Shields families would be the only two families to live their lives throughout the life of the official cove. There was always an Oliver and a Shields in the fields, tending homesteads, and harnessing water from the creeks. Other families came and went, would pop in and out, one generation stayed, the next one moved out, only for the next to return. The cove's beginnings, heyday, and demise would see the presence of these two steadfast families. But only one was there from the very start and remained there to the very end.

The first family of Cades Cove crossed through here for 119 years, from 1818-1937. John and Luraney Oliver would produce four hearty and loving generations, all raised in the cove, and each generation saw at least one portion of the valley's lifetime: the birth, flourishing, and ultimate death of the beautiful, fertile, isolated, and welcoming community. The most perfect land on earth. All lie peacefully buried in the small cemetery at the Primitive Baptist Church still covered with piles of flowers. A reminder that we cross through and over numerous places and phases in our lives, but certain crossings can only occur once. They are rare, profound. Those crossings reach beyond oneself to touch an entire community; can create an entire way of life. Such crossings, through surging creeks, storms, sunlit days, ridges, peaks and valleys ...those hard-fought crossings are never without meaning, purpose. Those crossings keep us moving forward, our roots and blooms reaching to where the eagles soar.

The eagle sat in its nest watching the people down in the valley. Letting out a squawk, it peered down on one smaller human, an Oliver boy, who was looking up into its eyes. Watching each other, the boy turned both sides of his mouth up, smiling at the majestic bird. The eagle could not swoop down because it was sitting on two eggs just hatched that afternoon. Feeling content and safe in its nest, she turned her head into her back feathers and went to sleep in the warm afternoon breezes of the cove. The boy watched the head of the eagle disappear, knowing it was safe, and readying a brand new life. He wished he could be there to see the baby eaglets appear; the male eagle would soon return to the huge nest with food. Nature always has a way. The boy smiled. The eagle rustled and opened one eye. Both animals looked at each other and marveled at the surrounding beauty they shared. Finally, both turned away from one another to cross through the last day enveloped in the crossing of warm breezes and ghostly memories of the community of Cades Cove.

About the Author

atherine Astl holds a Master's Degree in English Literature and Curriculum from Southern New Hampshire University, a Bachelor's in English from University of South Florida, and is a graduate of the International Summer Schools Shakespeare and Literature program at the University of Cambridge, Cambridge, England. She also holds an Associate of Science Degree in Legal Assisting and worked as a civil litigation trial paralegal for 27 years before switching to her current position teaching English Literature. Catherine is the author of two non-fiction books used in college/university paralegal programs throughout the country: *Behind the Bar-Inside the Paralegal Profession* and *Behind the Bar-From Intake to Trial,* as well as having authored over 25 published articles. Her two novels are: *Three Gates,* and *The Colonists.*

Oliver's Crossing is the author's fifth book, and third published novel. A lifelong writer and reader, Catherine is drawn to history, science, the classics, and historical fiction with compelling, deep-rooted relationships.

Catherine lives in Wesley Chapel, Florida. In her spare time, which is spare indeed, she spends time with her son and family, reads, writes, scrapbooks, exercises, travels, and scours bookshops to add to her personal library which is always expanding. She is hard at work on her next novel.

CPSIA information can be obtained
at www.ICGtesting.com
Printed in the USA
LVHW051629180322
713802LV00009B/447

9 781621 835783